T0283063

CARDALE JONES

CARDALE JONES

Leading the Buckeyes, Finding My Purpose, and Never Giving Up

CARDALE JONES
WITH BILL RABINOWITZ

Library of Congress Cataloging-in-Publication Data available upon request.

This book is available in quantity at special discounts for your group or organization. For further information, contact:

Triumph Books LLC
814 North Franklin Street
Chicago, Illinois 60610
(312) 337-0747
www.triumphbooks.com

Printed in U.S.A.
ISBN: 978-1-63727-530-6
Design and page production by Nord Compo
Images on insert page 7 (bottom) and page 8 are courtesy of the authors; all other images are courtesy of Getty Images.

CONTENTS

FOREWORD

Car. Dale. Jones.

Car. Dale. Jones.

12 Gauge, baby.

I've broadcast college sports for 30 years. I've been all over the world. Never in those 30 years of broadcasting have I seen a story as compelling as Cardale Jones's overnight stardom in leading Ohio State to the 2014 national championship.

I broadcast the Big Ten Football Championship Game for Fox. That early December night in Indianapolis is one I'll never forget. A young man from Cleveland, Ohio, was thrust into the spotlight at the most climactic time of the season for the world-famous Ohio State Buckeyes. Not only did he deliver, but he became a legend.

No one really knew who Cardale Jones was before that game. He'd been a seldom-used backup for two years. But when J. T. Barrett broke his ankle at the start of the fourth quarter against Michigan the week before, Cardale had to become the man.

When I opened the broadcast that night, it was obvious what the storyline was.

Car. Dale. Jones.

Car. Dale. Jones.

The whole state of Ohio is counting on Cardale Jones.

I didn't know Cardale's life story back then. All I knew was what Ohio State coaches had told me: that he was a big, strong guy with a huge arm. That he was a fun guy who all his teammates liked, and that he had talent. That he was a guy who came from the hood in Cleveland—the *hood* hood—and made it out of there. Buckeyes coach Urban Meyer told me he had a good feeling about him. He knew there was the potential for him to play well, and that there was no other choice. That was the most important thing to me. He *had* to play Cardale in the biggest game of the year, and the kid had to deliver.

Boy, did he. Cardale led the Buckeyes to a 59–0 rout of favored Wisconsin that got Ohio State into the first College Football Playoff.

A guy who'd never started a game looked like a pro. When he started airing it out, that's when I understood why his nickname was 12 Gauge. He had a cannon—with arc and distance and velocity and spin. He was clearly in the zone. I remember saying to myself, "How can it be that you haven't played all year, that you're the third-string quarterback, and you come in and have the game of your life?"

Then Cardale showed it wasn't a fluke by leading Ohio State to wins over Alabama and Oregon to win the national championship. It was the best three-game quarterbacking debut in the history of college football. We'd never seen anything like that before, and I doubt if we will ever see anything like that again. It was all or nothing for Cardale. Here was his shot. They didn't want to give him a shot. He'd gotten beat out. Now all of a sudden when it mattered most, Cardale Jones got an opportunity, and he turned in the greatest three-game debut ever.

But to distill Cardale Jones's life story to those three games is to miss the point. As impressive as that playoff run was, the bigger miracle is that he ever got the chance to shine, as you'll see from the rest of this book. His story is one of coming from humble beginnings, not having the support and means that many others had, but getting an opportunity through sports, especially when it came to his education. That's the kind of story you see quite often in African American homes, but you never see it get to the level to which Cardale took it. He had the heart and courage and mental capabilities to figure out what he needed to figure out in a very short time span when he hadn't played the whole year.

I felt his story. I connected with his story. I rooted for him internally to seize this moment because I knew it could change his life. His story is my favorite story of my career. Talk about triumph through adversity. Coaches and teachers always say, "Wait your turn. Stay above it. Be ready." He was all of those things. When he won that Wisconsin game, there was a tear of joy in my eye for him. It was like out of a movie.

But movies end and life goes on. Cardale began the 2015 season as the starter but was eventually benched even though the Buckeyes were undefeated. They should have let him continue to play until he lost. Urban is a friend of mine, a real friend, but I say to him, "You're the only coach I know who will bench a quarterback who never lost a game for you." He laughs. He's like, "You're right."

In the NFL, Cardale never got a real opportunity in Buffalo or with the Los Angeles Chargers. But I still think Cardale is a major success. He got his degree from Ohio State. He's got several business interests, including working on name, image, and likeness opportunities with current student-athletes.

Cardale is a winner. If you put him in a position to win, he's going to win. He has a gift, and that gift is his spirit. He also has an incredibly sharp mind and an engaging personality. There are some guys who you just want to be around, and he's one of them.

It's been almost a decade since Cardale led Ohio State to that unlikely championship, which seems hard to believe. To this day, people approach me and repeat my opening line from that Big Ten Football Championship Game. Even Urban Meyer. He'll come up to me and go, "Car. Dale. Jones. Car. Dale. Jones." I'm just grateful that I was able to have a small part in Cardale's story, one of the great college football stories of all time.

I love this kid. Stories like his are why I love what I do. He's what it's all about!

—Gus Johnson, Fox Sports announcer

PUBLISHER'S NOTE

This story belongs to Cardale Jones, but it is also told by many friends, family members, teammates, coaches, and others who have joined him along his path. Accounts from these individuals are set off in the narrative with alternate text.

INTRODUCTION

What just happened?

What just freaking happened?

That's the thought I had as I sat in the locker room at AT&T Stadium in Texas that Monday night in January 2015. I had been an afterthought for my entire Ohio State football career until just a few weeks earlier. What notoriety I had gained until then wasn't the kind any athlete would want.

Nobody thought I'd be in this position. Hell, a couple months earlier, I was already planning my departure from Ohio State, eager for a chance to prove myself as a quarterback elsewhere. Then my friend J. T. Barrett broke his ankle against Michigan in the rivalry game that always means the most to any Buckeye. I was thrust into a role that nobody thought I was ready for. But I knew I was.

I hadn't always followed the straight-and-narrow path. I hadn't always made it easy on myself or others. But I had already overcome so much: A tough upbringing in Cleveland as the youngest of six. I never knew who my father was. A far-from-perfect relationship with my mother.

I had dreamed of playing for Ohio State, only to have the coach who recruited me fired. Urban Meyer took over just as I was arriving, and I don't think I ever truly gained his trust—and vice versa.

Yet somehow we had reached the pinnacle. A 59–0 destruction of Wisconsin in my starting debut that propelled us into the first College Football Playoff. A 42–35 win over big, bad Alabama in the CFP semifinal in New Orleans. And now, on this Monday night, a 42–20 victory over Oregon for the national championship.

It was just such an indescribable feeling. So many times I'd wondered if all the struggles, hard work, and sacrifice would pay off. You have times during a season and during your career when you question that. You think about the workouts in the weight room when you feel you're pushed beyond your limit and you almost feel you're going to die. You think about the relationships with teammates and coaches. You think about the talks in the locker room, the jokes and the heart-to-hearts. You think about all the sacrifices you've endured together for a moment like this. We'd all overcome so much.

I was the last player left in our locker room when the magnitude of what I, and we, had accomplished washed over me. I reflected not just on my journey of the season but on my journey in life to get to that point. I had stared death in the face more than my fair share of times. I was supposed to be somewhere else. I was supposed to be back home in Cleveland cheering for Ohio State to win this game, not actually leading the Buckeyes to it. I remember as a 10-year-old in January 2003, when they were playing Miami for the national championship, watching with my family on TV as we cheered for Ohio State to win. Now I was there and knew there was a kid who'd watched me do this and now wanted to go to Ohio State because of what had just happened. Sitting in that locker room, I took a moment to reflect on it, and I couldn't help but think, *Wow, this really is crazy. If I hadn't endured all those hurdles, if I hadn't stuck it out when I didn't really want to, if anything at all had transpired differently, I wouldn't be here right now.*

What a journey it has been.

Chapter 1

MY EARLY YEARS

I WAS BORN in the front seat of my Uncle Dale's car.

That's how I got my name: Car. Dale.

I'm not joking.

Dale Murphy, uncle:

It's true. Cardale was born in my car, a 1986 Audi. I was visiting my pregnant sister Florence at our mom's house. I think at the time my sister was still living with my mother.

"I think I'm fixin' to have this baby," she told me.

"Girl, quit playin'," I said.

"For real."

"You've got to be kidding."

My mother lived on 123rd and Osceola in Cleveland. University Hospital is on 115th and Euclid, which is probably a three-minute drive, so I said, "Well, c'mon, I'll run you to the hospital."

By the time I turned the corner from 123rd to get to Superior Avenue, she was like, "You better hurry up! I think he's coming."

I was like, "Girl, please stop it!"

She was in the front seat and was wearing sweatpants. At the time, I was a fireman. I had training in emergency childbirth. I could have delivered him, but I didn't want to deliver my own sister's baby.

She wasn't really screaming like some women do in labor. This was her sixth baby, after all. But she was like, "Hurry up, hurry up! He's coming!"

I was like, "Girl, you better hold that."

But she couldn't. She just kind of leaned back from the edge of the front seat and lowered her sweatpants to her hips, and he came out inside her sweatpants.

Two minutes later, I got to the hospital. I went into the emergency room, and they said, "Is she in labor?" I said, "No, she done had the baby in my car!"

When I got back to my car, he was crying. I kept thinking, Oh my God, Oh my God, please don't let the afterbirth come in my car.

Her water did break in my car, but I was spared the afterbirth. They put my sister in a wheelchair to take her into the hospital with the baby, and I was like, "I've got to move my car." I think I went back to my mother's house and told her she'd had the baby.

I saw my sister maybe two days later. "By the way, what did you name the baby?" I asked.

She said, "Cardale."

At first, I didn't make the connection to my name and my car. I was like, "Cordell? Is that what you mean?"

When she repeated "Cardale," I said, "Why would you name him Cardale?"

She said, "Dale, because he was born in your car."

I was like, "Girl, you're crazy."

The funny thing is, if I hadn't been visiting my mom, she would have probably had to deliver the baby.

Thanks, Uncle Dale. Here's the funny thing: I have never asked my mom what my name would have been if I hadn't been born in Uncle Dale's car. If I'd been born 10 minutes later, I assume I'd be named something else. According to my Uncle Dale, I would have been named after my Uncle Audi, which would have been fitting, because that's the type of car I was born in.

That day, September 29, 1992, I became the last of my mom's six kids. She had her four oldest with William "Butch" Jones before having my brother Matt, who's older by a year and a day, and then me from different biological fathers. I never knew my dad, have no idea who he is, and never cared to try to find out. My mom decided to give Matt and me the Jones name so we'd all have the same last name.

That's a big family, but the seven of us were far outnumbered by our extended family that shared our 2,000-square-foot house on Osceola Avenue where I lived until I was in second grade.

There were about 20 of us in all. My grandparents, Naomi and Robert Murphy, had a bedroom downstairs. My uncles Tony and Dwayne shared the attic. Upstairs, my mom, my uncle Dale, and my aunt Lena and her three kids each had a bedroom. My five siblings and I shared one bedroom that had three bunk beds. The pile of clothes from all of us was so big that we'd play hide and seek in it.

I've been given a bunch of nicknames in my life—12 Gauge, C. J., and Sky 12 are just a few—but the one that my family calls me is Buster. I got that from my grandma because when I was a baby, I bounced around so much that I'd constantly bust out of my diaper or onesie. My siblings still call me that more often than they call me Cardale.

My sister Sheena is the oldest of my siblings. She felt like more of a mother than a sister. She was a protector and provider for all of us siblings. She's selfless and would give you her last dime. Next came my brother Javon, who we call Jay. Jay, a flight attendant, is super ambitious and very resourceful. He's always on the go, and you can't tell him no. Growing up, he was heavily into church and way more spiritual than the rest of us, more like my grandparents. He still is. When Jay was in middle school, he lived with our grandparents, so I'm pretty sure he got a lot of that from living in that household. Even before he became a flight attendant, we used to say he was the brokest guy in the world who could still manage to find a way to travel anywhere. He'd just pack his stuff, and the next thing you know, he'd be in a different country or in a different state staying with friends.

If I ever need to talk to someone who can give me answers to help me, I'll turn to Jay. If I ever just want to vent or bitch and know they'll have my back even if I'm wrong, I'll talk to my sisters. If I tell Sheena, "I ran a red light and the cop gave me a ticket," she'll say, "That dumbass cop! Why the fuck did he give you a ticket?" Jay's more like, "You ran a red light, and that's the consequence."

After Jay came Naomi, who we call "Nay Nay" to differentiate her from my grandmother. Nay Nay, like Sheena, is a beautician. She has no filter. Not at all. She and Sheena, if they don't approve of someone we're dating, they'll let us know in blunt terms. Neither of my sisters has kids, but if they did, they would be unbelievable moms, just from how they took care of us when we were young and how they interact with their nieces and nephews. Nay Nay is the firecracker of the family. She's tough love at times, but extremely loyal. When I was a kid, she'd curse me out, kick my ass and then turn around and make me some noodles.

Devonte, who's Dee for short, is my second-oldest brother, five years older than me. He is the best athlete in the family—or I should say that he was until I came along. Ha. He was a tight end and defensive end at Collinwood High School. Dee is adventurous; he loves to try new things. He's very outdoorsy. He loves to fish. I always called him crazy for taking his kayak out on a lake to fish. Dee would spend hours out there and would even get up in the middle of the night to do it. One time, he took me. I cast my line in the water twice without getting a fish to bite immediately. That was enough for me. I was ready to go. He just laughed. He's a lot more patient than I am.

The sibling closest to my age is Matthew, who's one year and one day older than I am. Despite our closeness in age, he couldn't be more different than me. He's the reason I don't believe in astrology. Outside of sports, we have little in common. Matthew has always been the kind of person who'd try to find a way around things. He's an entrepreneur who thinks outside the box and is firm in his convictions and is very prideful. All of us as siblings are all so different, so it's kind of weird that we all grew up in the same household. The one thing in common we had was my mom.

OK, where do I start about my mother? I don't want to be overly harsh, but I want to be real too. I wouldn't say my mom was *physically* absent as much as she was *emotionally* absent. Looking back on how things were, I think a lot of things that me and my siblings were going through could have been eased if she'd been emotionally supportive. Just a simple "Everything is going to be OK" from her would have been so reassuring. I know she loved me, but I can probably count on two hands the number of times she actually said, "I love you"—and that's being generous.

Sometimes she would embarrass me publicly in front of my friends. "Shut the fuck up," she'd say. One thing that always stood out like a sore thumb to me was that she would say, "If I knew then what I know now, I'd have six dogs instead of six kids."

Don't get me wrong—there was love in our family, but love was just always inferred. I had plenty of love and support from my siblings. We always looked out for each other. But we all felt some form of neglect from our mom that we never talked about. We had enough on our plate dealing with the everyday hardships that come with growing up underprivileged in the inner city. There was no point in talking about feelings. We just rolled with the punches and dealt with whatever life had to throw at us together. Expressing personal feelings and emotions just wasn't something we did. It almost would have felt like an unspoken sign of weakness in our household.

Things that are common in others' homes didn't happen in ours. Bedtime stories, good-night kisses, tucking us in? No way. More like, "Go the fuck to bed" or, "Take y'all asses to sleep." Discipline was often handled physically. In this day and age, if you whack a kid, it's considered child abuse. My mom would probably be in jail for the shit she did to us. She'd fuck us up: belts, fists, switches, extension cords—anything you can name. I remember one time when my sister Nay Nay was doing her hair, I took one of her bobby pins and stuck it in an electrical socket. Poof! It shocked the shit out of me. I was old enough to know not to do it, and my mom kicked my ass. We all got our asses kicked a lot, especially me and my brothers when we used to fight. I was the youngest, so I'd usually get my ass kicked anyway, and I'd be like, "I know I'm going to get my ass kicked for fighting, so I've already lost."

I also know my mom used drugs. Other than weed, she'd never do it in front of us. But did we know she was doing it? Yeah. We weren't stupid. I do remember being older and seeing her buy crack one time. I don't know if it's true or not, but she said, "Oh, this isn't for me." My mom wasn't alone in our neighborhood.

Tony Murphy, uncle:

When I was growing up there, the neighborhood was nice. Everyone called it the 123rd because that was the main street through it. It wasn't a rich area, but people took care of their homes and lawns. We had a laundromat. We had dry cleaners. We had grocery stores. We had the 123 Mini Mart, the corner store where everyone would hang out. We were always taught to respect our elders. When we'd see Miss Johnson or Miss Davis or Miss Daniels carrying their grocery bags down the street, we'd run over and carry their bags because we knew we were going to get a quarter or 50 cents as a tip. The whole street was full of kids and grandkids. Everybody knew everybody.

Then crack hit the scene in the 1980s and especially the '90s, and the neighborhood seemed like it went from sugar to shit overnight. The older people were afraid to come out because drug dealers were everywhere. Crackheads were everywhere. Then it got so bad that there were drive-bys. People robbing drug dealers. The basketball courts we used to hang out at were full of drug dealers. People were smoking crack all around. And I was one of those guys. I had a horrible addiction. Thankfully, somehow Cardale didn't get caught up in it.

We moved five times when I was a kid after leaving the house on Osceola, but all the houses or apartments were in the same neighborhood. Money was always tight. My mom worked as a home health aide and braided hair for additional income. We grew up on government assistance at times—food stamps, WIC, you name it. We needed all the help we could get. I'm pretty sure I had friends who were in a similar situation or had it even worse, but it wasn't good. I remember going to bed hungry because the monthly food stamp card hadn't gone into effect yet. We didn't have a washer or dryer, so I'd wear clothes multiple days. I didn't know you were supposed to change your drawers every day. If I had a stain on my shirt, I'd wear it backward so it wasn't that noticeable and I wouldn't be mocked. When we did wash our clothes, it was usually with bar soap in a sink or bathtub, and then we'd hang them up to dry. I don't know if we ever had more than one set of linens.

> *Jay Jones, brother:*
>
> *An addiction is an illness, and it's sometimes hard to accept that. Because of the addiction, we didn't have the best childhood. I never had a Christmas where I got what I wanted. For a lot of families that are on fixed incomes, it's like, "OK, you can pick out one thing that you want, and I'll make sure you get it." That was never the case for us. I never remember getting the gift I wanted for Christmas. Gifts were always, "This is a board game for all of y'all," or something that came from a charity. We probably wouldn't have had anything if it wasn't for that.*

I was always tall for my age and grew steadily. That meant I'd quickly outgrow my clothes. But we didn't have the money to get me new ones. My clothes were always hand-me-downs from my brothers. I'd take a shoestring and use that as a belt if the pants were too big.

Shoes were another issue. I remember my toes scrunching into the ends of them when I outgrew them. I'd cut the ends off shoes so I could wear them for longer. In school, I'd just take them off during class so my feet weren't cramped. If I had a sleepover with friends, I knew my shoes had a horrible odor, so I'd keep them on until my friends went to sleep. During the long, snowy Cleveland winters, we couldn't afford boots, so I'd take a plastic bag and wrap them over my shoes to try to keep my feet dry.

Even with the issues with my mom, the whole Murphy side of the family was close, especially when I was young. I had a great relationship with my extended family, especially my uncles Tony and Dale. I was also close to my grandparents, who had 13 children. My grandparents eventually moved out of the house on Osceola to one around the corner, and I would often hang out with them in their garden or with my grandfather's friends. My grandma is the one who taught me to clean. She had a lot of health issues from having diabetes. She eventually lost part of one leg and most of her vision. But even in a wheelchair, she would keep her house spotless. Often, I would go over and help her clean her bathroom and kitchen. She taught me how to deep-clean a house, which is something I still do to this day.

I remember as she got older, I'd think, *What would happen if she passed away? How would the family be?* Because she was the glue. She reminded me of the movie *Soul Food*: The grandma, Big Mama, was the heart of the family. When that character died, the family splintered. My grandma did pass away when I was in third grade, and what happened in the movie is kind of what happened to us. We used to have these huge get-togethers all the time. There was less and less of that. I remember visiting my grandfather after that, and when I walked by his bedroom, I could see he still kept my grandma's side of the bed made.

My first two memories as a kid both happened before I entered kindergarten. The first came in the spring when I went to a park with some older cousins. Their dad, Maurice, was called Big Mo because he was about 6'4" and weighed 260 pounds. He was pushing my cousins on a swing, and these weren't gentle little pushes. They were going so high it looked like they'd flip over the bar. He called it "shooting to the moon." That looked like fun to me. I pleaded with him, "Shoot me to the moon too!" The problem was, I was really skinny then. So he was pushing me and pushing me, and all of a sudden I really did go above the bar and flip over. I was scared shitless, and as I went back around the bar, I let go and got sent flying. Unfortunately, I didn't land on just dirt or grass. A brick happened to be there, and *bam*, the back of my head landed right on it, which knocked me out.

I'm pretty sure I had a concussion. When I came to, Big Mo was carrying me on his shoulder, rushing to get me home. He'd packed my head with mud to stop the bleeding. When he got to our house and my mom saw me, she started freaking out. The next thing I knew, I was in the hospital and on my stomach as they stitched up my head. They needed two layers of skin to do it.

Not long after that came the second memory—a bicycle accident. In our family, we were taught to ride a bike at an early age. Our uncles used to say, "Get those training wheels off. You don't need those things." But no one taught me how to brake. One day I was flying down the sidewalk about to turn left in front of our neighbor Miss Daniels's house on the corner. Before I could really react, I saw the stop sign in front of me. Unable to swerve out of the way, I smacked into that stop sign so hard. We had people at our house that day for a fish fry. Music was playing loud. But there happened to be a pause between songs at the moment I collided with the stop sign, so everyone heard it. *Bam!* I tried to play it off at first by laughing. But then reality—and the pain—hit. I just started crying.

Can you tell I was an adventurous kid? I knew where the line was and always kind of flirted with it. I know I tested my mom's patience. The most dangerous thing I ever did was in eighth grade. My middle school, Patrick Henry, was in the process of being demolished and was half torn down. One of my cousins knew that scavengers would go to the school and take copper and other scraps and get money for them. My brother Matt, our friend Chuck, and I decided to go check it out. We were climbing through the rubble and exploring other parts of the school. Eventually we made our way to the top of the three-story building. The edge of the roof was about two feet wide. Of course, we decided to see who could walk the longest on that edge. If you fell to the left, no problem—that was the roof. But there was absolutely nothing to the right. If you fell that way, you'd be dead. Seriously. There was nothing but rubble and pavement underneath. Then, just to push things, we challenged each other to run on this edge. Fortunately, none of us fell to the right.

So yeah, like most kids, I did my share of stupid stuff. In the winter, we would throw snowballs at cars, sometimes with eggs in them. Other times, we'd throw rocks. One time, we did that at a car behind Second Lakeview Baptist Church. The driver stopped, grabbed a gun, and started shooting at us. We took off running for our lives, not knowing if he was shooting in the air just to scare us or really trying to put bullet holes in a few 13-year-olds.

As my uncle Tony said, gunfire was common in my neighborhood. Usually it was just people shooting in the air, but I knew several people who were shot to death. I had a friend named LaSalle who was killed on the west side of Cleveland when we were in high school. Ant Gordon, who was a year or two older than me, was another guy who was killed. He was expected to be the next big thing. I remember the emotional toll that death took on our community and all of the kids who looked up to Ant.

JayJay Robinson, friend:

Growing up where we come from, there's so many wrong paths we could turn down. In our neighborhood, there was a lot of gun violence, a lot of drug violence, a lot of gangs. Especially where we were, we were surrounded by gangs. Honestly, I don't know how Cardale didn't become a part of a gang. Where he lived, there was nothing but gang activity. For him to keep on his straight-and-narrow path and never fall into that is great. He was never drunk, never smoked, never in gangs. It's incredible to be from the neighborhood we're from and not ever to have partaken in any of that.

I just never had any interest in that stuff because I saw the effect it had on people in my neighborhood, in my family. Even in college I only got fucked up on alcohol one time. I just didn't want to ingest anything that would make me feel different. I'd seen people who were functional alcoholics, and I'd seen people so drunk they pissed on themselves. I'd seen people drunk who did stupid things and people who were high and did stupid things. People who stuck needles in their arms—I'd seen how their bodies looked after they got hooked. I didn't want to look like that. I didn't want to be like that.

I did have a few other close calls with gun violence, though. One was on a night after a school dance, when I was out with three friends. Back then, the style was to wear oversized clothes. On our way to parties or dances, we'd stop at gas stations to buy white tees. Even though I was so skinny, I always wanted a 2XL shirt, but at that time, the gas station on 110th and Lakeview only had 4XL left, so that's what I bought. The bigger the shirt, the more stylish and swaggy I thought I was. On the way home from the dance, some guy got out of his car and started shooting at us. I had—and still to this day have—no clue why. As we took off running, I remember looking back to see if he was shooting in the air, but no, I recall seeing the muzzle flash in our direction, hearing the bullets fly past, and seeing them skip off the ground. We were hauling ass, freaking out, like, "What the hell is going on?" When I got home, I looked at my new, fresh white T-shirt and there were two bullet holes in it—one on the side and the other through the torso. The shirt was so big that the guy missed me, but I was still like, "That's crazy!" That made me think about a lot of things as far as going out and partying, I can tell you that.

But the scariest incident with a gun happened when I was 15. I was at home one night sitting in my bed playing video games. A family friend was in the house. He had a handgun and pulled it out to place it on the sink as he used the restroom, which shared the same wall as my room. I had just gotten my very first cell phone (more on that later), and I had plugged it into its charger. I thought I had gotten a text message and leaned over to check the phone. At that moment, I heard a loud bang. The gun had fired. It must have had an extremely light trigger, because it went off when the guy picked it up to put it back in his pants. I remember thinking, *What the heck was that?* The first thing I looked at was the window, thinking someone had shot from outside, but there was no bullet hole there. Then I saw one in the wall that my room shared with the bathroom. The bullet had traveled through that wall and out the back of the house, exiting right where I had been sitting. If I hadn't been leaning over to look at my phone that bullet would have hit me right in the face. The odd thing was, I hadn't actually gotten a text.

This was my life then. But somehow I always believed I was destined for something better. I just didn't know the path yet.

Chapter 2

FALLING IN LOVE WITH SPORTS

SPORTS WERE ALWAYS A BIG PART of my family's life. I grew up listening to stories about how talented my uncles were and their glory days on the local courts and fields. But they never had a chance to pursue their athletic dreams past high school. My brother Matt was really good at basketball. I remember going to Devonte's high school football games and seeing how proud people were of him. He'd catch a pass and run down the sideline, and my mom would run along the sideline with him. That was really the first time I saw that my mom was proud of us, honestly. I'm pretty sure she had other moments when she was proud, but she just rarely displayed it.

So I thought, *Cool, I'm gonna try football.* It wasn't that I was forced to play football, but I had to do something in the summer to keep busy. My mom wanted to know we weren't just running the streets 24/7. But I wasn't that great at it, and I definitely wasn't a quarterback. In fact, I never really thought of myself as a good athlete until high school, even though I, like many inner-city Black kids, figured sports would be my best opportunity for a better life. Coaches had me play on the offensive line because I was tall. I admit I was super lazy because I didn't know what position I really wanted to play.

But despite all that, I loved football, and we had a really good team—the Glenville Titans, a Pop Warner organization in the Cleveland Muny League started by Rob McQueen, better known as Rob Jay. He was a local hero to many. He played at Glenville back in the day, and he started the Titans. Without Rob Jay, many great players who went on to play at Glenville and other high schools around the city wouldn't have had a good foundation within athletics. He instilled teamwork, accountability, dedication, and sacrifice in us at an early age. My first two years with the Titans, we were coached by Darnell Williams and Tom Owens. We went 22–0 and won back-to-back city championships. The same core of players played together all the way through my senior year of high school. We had the same uniform colors—red and black—as the Glenville Tarblooders, the high school team. In our own little world, we were a big deal.

I loved being on the Titans as much for the camaraderie as for the fun of playing. I'm still close to a lot of the guys from those teams—Johnny "JayJay" Robinson, Rob Waltson Jr., Andrew "Tank" Sturdivant, and others. We'd go to JayJay's house and have the biggest sleepovers sometimes during the season. But sometimes when we had guys close to the weight limit, the night before games, we would stay at Coach Dar's house just to make sure we made weight. Some might look at that as a punishment, but we always did team-building activities such as going bowling, going to an arcade, or attending local high school games together.

JayJay's parents, Francine and Johnny Robinson Sr., were awesome. His older brothers played at Glenville at the time, and JayJay's parents would take us to his games. When I'd go to visit friends, it was obvious that many of them had things I didn't. Many had both parents; I barely had one. They always had new shoes. They had cell phones. They had washers and dryers, so their clothes were always clean. I had none of these things. But I wasn't really jealous of the things they had. I'm not sure why, other than that, to me, the way we lived was the only thing I knew. That was my norm. I also probably wasn't jealous because my friends' families treated me like I was their own kid at times. They made sure I ate, gave me hand-me-downs, and performed other kind gestures that made me feel cared for. I think they knew my family and our economic situation and helped me out when they could. I'll never forget one thing JayJay's dad did for me. One year we got these cool jackets that resembled the Tarblooders varsity jackets. They had our Pop Warner logo and read GLENVILLE TITANS on the back with our names on them. With a $100-$150 payment, Big Johnny would take your order and have your jacket for you in a week. No way my family could afford that. I didn't even ask my mom, because I already knew the answer. But the Robinsons paid for my jacket, and that was like the coolest thing I ever had. I was always hesitant to wear it because I didn't want to mess it up.

JayJay Robinson:

When it was announced that we'd get the jackets, Cardale didn't even have a reaction. He acted like he wasn't interested in it because he knew he wasn't going to be able to come up with that type of money. He wasn't even trying to be a part of the conversation. As a kid, when you know your parents can't afford a jacket, deep down you feel a certain type of way. You might not say anything to anybody, but your feelings are hurt. When my parents told him they'd get him a jacket, he was extremely excited. You could see his face light up, smiling with those big ol' cheeks. He was already a big part of the team, but to be able to get that jacket made him feel even more a part of it.

Later on, I wore the jacket to the Glenville Rec Center and took it off when I got in a basketball game. Someone stole it, though I didn't realize it right away. When I realized it was missing, I wondered if I'd just misplaced it somewhere in my house. I was crushed. Then, months later, my sister Nay Nay saw a kid walking down the street with my jacket. She knew it was mine because my name was on the chest. She told me she whipped this kid's ass, biting his fingers as she had him on the ground trying to get his hand uncuffed from the sleeves on the jacket. After all that, she finally got the jacket off the kid and returned it to me with a few minor rips from the scuffle.

For me, football wasn't just another sport to play. I loved it. I didn't get a lot of attention because I was a lineman, but I still enjoyed dominating up front. I knew my role and was good at it. I felt it was almost a guaranteed touchdown if we ran to my side. But as we got older, I didn't know if I had a future in football. I'd go to high school games and see that linemen were so much bigger than I was. I was tall but skinny. With my frame, I didn't think I could get heavy enough to play on the line. No way did I even *want* to get that big. The idea of switching positions that late, especially to quarterback, didn't really occur to me. I'd played offensive line my whole life up to that point, and I was going to play a different position in high school? Nope. I was content to stick to baseball. I was a pitcher and a first baseman. I felt that in baseball, I had more control over the outcome of games. As an offensive lineman in football, I could have a great game and we could still lose. In baseball, on the other hand, rarely does a pitcher dominate and his team still loses. I had a couple no-hitters in my day. By the time I was in eighth grade, I could throw 83 mph. Few kids that age could hit pitches that fast.

In fact, I thought I wouldn't play high school football at all, even though all my friends and I had talked about it for years. We'd gone to different middle schools, and it was our dream to play together at

Glenville High School for legendary coach Ted Ginn Sr. But I didn't want to play on the line. I'd get killed.

I definitely didn't want to play my ninth grade year for Glenville. We didn't have a freshman team, only JV. In Muny League, we had three levels, depending on age: Midget was for ages 8–10, Pee-Wee for 11–13, and Bantamweight for 14–15. Bantamweight was mostly for eighth graders and freshmen who didn't turn 16 years old before the season. I decided to play Bantamweight. The first year, I played on the offensive line and didn't really enjoy it. But the quarterbacks coach on that team, Kevin Shorts, saw potential in me. He made a comment that I could be the quarterback on the Bantamweight team next year, my freshman year of high school. I was skeptical. I was like, "Whatever, dude. To go from the offensive line to quarterback, that ain't gonna happen."

That summer, I'd go by Glenville High School's football stadium, Robert "Bump" Taylor Field, on my way to baseball practice and see my buddies in camp for the Tarblooders. They'd jokingly rip me for not being on their team. They'd say, "You suck!" or "You ain't gonna play!" and things like that. But sometimes I'd stop and play catch with them after they were done. Just messing around. One day, I was at midfield, got on my knees, and launched the ball 50–60 yards and through the goalpost—just bombed it. Coach Ginn saw me and was like, "Who the hell is that? Come here." He knew my family. He was like, "You're a Murphy? Get the ball. Throw it again." I remember him telling the other players, "That's your quarterback right there."

JayJay Robinson:

I was there. Everybody just went, "Wow, did he really just do that?" Once everybody saw that and saw how far he could throw and how hard he could throw it, that's when they started wanting him to be the quarterback. People still talk about it to this day. We had

> *another kid who played quarterback the whole time growing up, but once we saw Cardale do that, we knew he was the one.*

It was so awkward because the quarterback on our team from Pop Warner on up was Devon Drish. His brother played quarterback at Glenville High. He felt he was destined to follow in his brother's footsteps, and so did we. Certainly I didn't think I'd take that job. I'd never even played the position.

I still was reluctant to play for the school team because I didn't want to play on the line. But Coach Ginn knew my uncle Tony, who was and still is a US Navy recruiter. He'd overcome his crack addiction, joined the military at age 34, and turned his life around. Uncle Tony pulled up to our house soon after in his US Navy van and was like, "C'mon, you're going to practice." We had a conversation about playing football and striving to be my best in whatever I did. As we talked, I got the sense that him asking me to go to practice was more like an order than an invitation. So I went. "This is where you should be," my uncle said. I started going to practice and workouts with those guys, and the rest is pretty much history.

It wasn't until midway through my freshman season at Glenville that I realized that I might have a real future in football. I was still so raw. In practice, I was late with the ball and just muscled it there. I threw like the baseball pitcher I still considered myself to be. I didn't really know how to play quarterback. I had talent and could do certain things, and I could always process information at a decent rate. Tony Overton—Coach Tone, we called him—was the coach of the JV team, and he talked to me after a loss about some of the things I was doing. He explained how I was late on some passes and that I was overthinking things and couldn't always rely on my athletic ability. That's when I started to really try to understand more of the game when it came to being a quarterback and being cerebral. That's when it really became more enjoyable to me. We'd talk about a certain coverage that we might get on a play, and Coach Tone would say things such as, "Hey, look, this might be open if you see this" or, "You can check for this if you see this." It wasn't always about dropping back and throwing to the open guy. It was the chess-like part of the game that I found I really enjoyed. That's what Coach Tone brought out in me at an early age.

The heart of Glenville's program was Coach Ginn. I knew of him at an early age when his son, Ted Ginn Jr., was a local star wide receiver (who went on to star at Ohio State and in the NFL). Ted Ginn Sr. was much more than a football coach. In 2007 he established the Ginn Academy in Cleveland, an all-boys charter school that was the first of its kind in northeast Ohio, and that's the school I attended. Discipline is a big part of Ginn Academy. Its mission is to develop exemplary students who will reach their full potential and develop and enhance their own self-worth.

Eric Lichter, personal trainer and former Ohio State strength coach:

In 2000 Ted Ginn Sr. walked into the Euclid sports training facility that I'd just opened with my business partner, Tim Robertson. We'd just put a press release in the local newspaper, and Ted Ginn Sr. saw it. We were literally painting the walls of our gym ourselves because, like any young entrepreneur, we couldn't afford to hire anyone else to do it. So Ted came in and had Pierre Woods, a 6'4", 240-pound linebacker who would play for Michigan, with him. Ted said, "I read the article. I've been a security guard at Cleveland

Glenville and I just got the head football coaching job, and I need help. I need to create a platform to train these kids and to help them, because if I don't, they're going to end up dead. I don't care about how many football games we win; I care about how many lives I save."

That's what Ted Ginn Sr.'s message was, and we spent four hours that day talking about training and how we could help. That was the start of our relationship. It was me and Tim and Ted Ginn Sr. and the men in the community such as Ronnie Bryant, who he still has there today. The first van that ever pulled up had Ted Ginn Jr. as a seventh grader, with Troy Smith and Donte Whitner and Dareus Hiley. All these Glenville guys who've gone to Ohio State. There are 30, 40, or 50 now who have been in the NFL, but there are thousands who have gone on to college who you'll never hear about who are not casualties of war up here.

I did not want to go to Ginn Academy. I had always thought I'd go to Glenville. That was my dream. I wanted to go to Glenville and play for the Tarblooders. And I also wanted to be around high school girls. But Coach Ginn tricked me and some of the other guys. He told us if we didn't go to Ginn Academy, we couldn't play for Glenville. Even though that doesn't make sense logically, I believed him, even though Ginn Academy athletes did play for Glenville because Ginn did not have its own sports programs. I still wanted to go to Glenville full-time.

At Ginn Academy, you had to wear dress clothes—a blazer with a button-down shirt, a necktie, and nice shoes. Problem was, my mom couldn't afford that. That summer, I did odd jobs for relatives to earn some extra money. I collected cans that I crushed to fill about eight huge trash bags that I could get some cash for at a local scrapyard. My relatives generously chipped in for the rest, including school supplies.

Ted Ginn Sr.:

I started Ginn Academy for a lot of reasons. I saw people didn't have expectations for kids because they weren't getting the right information about them. A cookie-cutter education isn't good. My philosophy for Ginn Academy is based on scholarship, leadership, and service. It's about love, passion, understanding. We're gonna love the kids, have passion with it, and give them proper understanding. You've got to give each kid their own individual plan, because they're all different. They're all at risk. With kids like Cardale, to deal with him, you had to deal with his life, his family, his upbringing. The school is there to give each kid an individual life plan—to love him, to get to know him, to find out what they're good at and help them navigate the world.

At Ginn Academy, we had a creed that we spoke in our auditorium every morning: "Our mission is to become exemplary students who will reach our full potential and beyond. We will recognize our genius and realize our self-worth. We will stay patient and poised to seize every opportunity for success. We are guided by scholarship, leadership, and service to all."

I can't say whether the academics at Ginn Academy were necessarily better than at Glenville or other Cleveland public schools. I didn't attend Glenville. I have no way to compare them. But because Ginn Academy was smaller—72 in my graduating class—I think the teachers were more invested and hands-on with students, and we were able to learn more life lessons. Who's easier to reach, 3 students who probably don't know what they're going to eat tonight, or 300?

I joke around with Coach Ginn sometimes about how he tricked me into attending his school, but I think he's the closest thing to a saint I can think of: Selfless. Relentless. Clearly a man of faith. Passionate. His passion has never been about the game of football. His passion really has been for saving lives. He's doing it through football. He saved mine and many more like me. He did an unbelievable job of giving guys motivation and examples of life more than anything. He cared about the lessons you learn through wins and losses, success and failure, more than the actual scoreboard. He's all about the bigger picture when it comes to being a coach. He's still a tough coach and believes that the way you carry yourself on the field translates to life and the real world.

He had a lot of molding to do with me. I remember my freshman year at the Ginn Academy. One special thing about the school was that it had people called linkage coordinators. They'd help teachers bond with students, assisting with behavioral issues if needed. The one for my class was named Brian Simmons, and sometimes I'd delight in tormenting him. I had a friend, and we'd call each other at night and say, "How are we going to piss off Simmons tomorrow?" One time we agreed to stage a fight with each other in class. Sure enough, halfway through class the next day, I reached over and yanked his tie. He grabbed mine, and we were swinging at each other, causing a ruckus, falling over chairs. I got kicked out of class, but my friend didn't, so I was like, "What's going on? This is BS!" I sure used some more foul language. The classroom was at the front of the building, and as I was walking out of the room backward, flashing double birds, I bumped into some guy who had just entered the building, who looked at me like,

"What the hell is wrong with this kid, and where the hell am I?" I proceeded to the principal's office, but at that time the principal, Ms. Ray, was dealing with other pressing matters, so she sent me to Coach Ginn's office. Well, who was in there but that man I'd bumped into moments earlier. It turned out it was Stan Drayton, who was at the time an assistant coach at Tennessee and would later become running backs coach at Ohio State under Urban Meyer. I was like, "Oh my God." Coach Ginn said something to me like, "You can't keep doing this shit." Coach Drayton said to me, "I'm here recruiting Mike Edwards, but Coach Ginn already told me you have potential to be a great player. You never know if we're going to cross paths again."

At the end of my Glenville career, I played in the Big 33 All-Star game for Ohio against Pennsylvania in Hershey, Pennsylvania, and players from Ohio met at the Woody Hayes Athletic Center at The Ohio State University to depart for Hershey for the week. That's when I learned Coach Drayton was on the OSU staff. When I saw him in the Woody Hayes parking lot in OSU gear, I thought to myself, *You've got to be kidding me.* "I remember you from when you were a freshman at Ginn Academy," Drayton said. "I remember you too," I said, embarrassed, as I vividly recalled our first encounter. It all had come full circle. Pretty funny, actually. Coach Ginn might have mentioned me to Coach Drayton that day in his office, but back then I was far from polished as a player and student.

The hits that came with playing quarterback were new to me. I got a false sense of security in practice that first year because quarterbacks were off-limits to hits. All I had to worry about was dropping back and delivering the ball downfield. It almost made me forget that tackling is part of the game. I found that out in my first JV game. We played our rival, St. Ignatius, one of the top programs in the state. I must have gotten sacked 10 times and hit another 15. It felt like three Wildcats were about to kill me every time I dropped back. It made me rethink not only whether I wanted to keep playing quarterback but whether my teammates even liked me. I was convinced my offensive linemen were missing blocks on purpose. As you probably figured out, we lost.

After we watched the film as a team, Coach Tone and I took a deep dive into the film. He pointed out all my many mistakes, to the point I felt he was blaming me for our failure. But I did understand that I was new to the position and had so much to learn. Coach Tone taught me how to study film, the need to have a short memory, to stay cool under pressure. Most of all, he preached the importance of being a leader, the one who teammates could turn to for guidance and reassurance when things weren't going well. As my freshman season progressed, so did my play. All the fears and worries I had leading into the season started to fade away. Learning the mental side of the game made the position more challenging but exciting. I enjoyed beating a defense mentally on an audible to convert a third down just as much as avoiding a sack and throwing a 50-yard touchdown.

By the end of my sophomore year, when I served as the backup on varsity as well as the JV starter, I really started to feel like a true quarterback. Going into my junior year, I had a good chance to win the starting varsity quarterback spot. I played in a lot of games as a sophomore on varsity during mop-up duty, which gave me valuable experience. If I became the starting varsity quarterback, I'd be succeeding Terrance Owens, who was graduating and getting ready to start his career at the University of Toledo. I thought I had matured, and in a lot of ways I had, but I still had more growing up to do. I still didn't quite grasp the bigger picture.

I remember what Terrance said to me after the last game of the season: "Cardale, I'm handing it over to you now, and you've got to wake up and understand what's on the line here for you, your career, this program, and this community," he said. He singled me out in front of the whole team, saying, "It's your team now." I took that to heart. That sophomore year was a pivotal one for me, and not only because of a blossoming football career.

Chapter 3

MORE THAN A MENTOR

As much as Coach Ginn helped me, he had a school to run and a Glenville team to coach and mentor. But he knew I needed special guidance. One of my Glenville teammates was Christian Bryant, who was a year older. He'd go on to be a star defensive back at Ohio State and play in the NFL. His brother, Coby, was the 2021 winner of the Jim Thorpe Award, given to college football's top defensive back, and was a first-round NFL draft pick in 2022. The Bryants' dad, Ronnie, was an assistant coach at Glenville. His wife had a cousin, Michelle Nash, who had always had a soft spot for kids. Michelle was unable to have any of her own because of ovarian cysts discovered when she was 17. She said that was the hardest thing she ever had to deal with. Michelle ran a home day-care business and had worked with youth in the Cuyahoga County juvenile detention system. Michelle was raised by her grandparents and had been a caregiver for her grandfather, who had recently died. She'd told Ronnie long before that she'd be happy to help if there was a kid they thought needed help. Coach Bryant and Coach Ginn thought she could help me.

Ronnie Bryant:

Ginn and I talked, and we knew it was utterly important to get some structure around Cardale. We weren't necessarily trying to replace his mom or anything like that. But like with any child, it's been proven that the better the support system, the better the outcome. So when Ginn approached me on the field, we probably looked over at Cardale, and he was being a goofball as usual. We laughed and agreed that, "Yeah, we've gotta get him somebody." I remember it like it was yesterday. Ginn looked at me and said, "Man, you've got to help me with this one." I said, "C'mon, man. You know I will. I'm gonna go home and pray on this situation." Then Michelle came into my mind. Michelle had a day care, and every child who ever came into contact with Michelle fell in love with her, from the smallest to the oldest. She just had that authenticity. I often say that kids have a built-in sensor, and it's attracted to authenticity. She was that person. I called Michelle and said, "I need you to do something. I need you to come to the field and meet this young man. I need you to just be in his life and support him." I didn't say to take his mother's place. That was certainly not my intent at all.

Coach Bryant mentioned Michelle to me one day and then introduced us the next day during a football practice in August 2008. "Hi, I'm Cardale," I said nonchalantly, not wanting to feel like some charity case. Coach Bryant had explained to me the previous day what Michelle's intentions were after he gave her some background on my upbringing and living situation. I was skeptical of her. *This lady only wants to get to know me because*

I'm a football player, I thought. I'd had a handful of people like this in my life after I started to show some potential as a player. They always seemed to show up during football season. They'd offer to buy me cleats or something like that. I looked at them suspiciously. I was just starting to sense that I had a future in football. I thought these new people were only trying to get close to me for what I might eventually be able to do for them or so they could say that they knew me before I became big. I didn't want any part of that.

That's the attitude I had when I met Michelle. In my mind, I wasn't willing to give our relationship a fighting chance. But I was hungry after practice, and she and her friend Angie took me to dinner at Subway. Michelle drove me back to her home in Euclid about 15 minutes away. We talked about my neighborhood because she'd grown up nearby on 118th Street.

The more we got to know each other, the more she learned about my struggles. I was so lacking in many basic necessities that she took me shopping, even though I found out that wasn't her original intention. She got me food after practices, new shoes, new cleats, new clothes, and even my first cell phone, which I mentioned earlier. After we'd eat and wash my clothes (she had a washing machine and a dryer!) and watch TV—cable for the first time!—she'd drive me home. Michelle wanted to meet my mom. Sometimes, she'd wait for hours in hopes of meeting her. Michelle was uncomfortable dropping me off without my mother being around, but I assured her that it was normal. Not seeing our mom all night wasn't a big deal for me and my siblings. I was grateful for what Michelle was doing for me, but my suspiciousness of her didn't immediately disappear. I still wondered if she'd be another person who'd leave my life after just a brief time. *Let me just ride this gravy train as long as I can*, I thought.

> *Michelle Nash:*
>
> *I remember my sister and I took him to the mall because he needed some shoes. I know you don't usually do that when you start mentoring. But he needed some shoes on his feet. He just had flip-flops, and they were completely torn up. I took him to the Foot Locker at Richland Mall. I told him to pick out a pair of tennis shoes and then thought to myself,* Why did I do that? *because I know these kids love these expensive tennis shoes. Cardale picked up a $69 pair of white Nikes. I'll never forget it. He didn't go for the expensive, expensive tennis shoes. He went right to these little white Nikes that he wanted. I asked what his shoe size was, and he told me, "Like a 9." The young man who was working in the store looked at me and shook his head, like "No way." I said, "Cardale, get your foot measured." The worker measured his feet. He was a size 12. I asked him, "When was the last time you got your foot measured?" He said, "I don't remember the last time I had a new pair of shoes." I walked out and I left him there with my sister and ran to the bathroom because I just got kind of emotional and I didn't want him to see it.*

Remember that incident when the gun with the hair trigger went off in the bathroom across from my bedroom and the bullet almost hit me? That happened only a couple weeks after I met Michelle. For me, that was pretty much the last straw. I called her up and asked her to get me. I grabbed a plastic grocery bag and filled it with my stuff, probably including some of my brother's as well. It was pretty late at night, maybe 2:00 AM, and I waited outside for her to pick me up. She took me to school the next morning, and it felt like I had a new vibe about myself. Part of it was that I didn't have to catch the bus, but part of it felt like I'd begun a new chapter of my life.

Michelle Nash:

I took him home, and the next day, I told Coach Ginn, "He's here. I don't know exactly what to do." Coach Ginn told me to keep calling his mother. But she never answered the phone. This went on for the longest. I talked to his uncle Tony, who knew Cardale was with me. I thought he would probably take Cardale. But he did not. I told my sister that I couldn't have him sleeping on my couch. We went and bought him an air mattress, and he slept on that for a couple weeks, but he was too tall for that. I had an extra bedroom, so when Cardale was at school, me, my sister, and Angie went out and got him a bedroom set and decorated the room. When he came home, he was quiet. As he sat on the bed, I asked, "What are you thinking?" And he said, "I've never had a room of my own." Once again, I left the room and went upstairs to my room and teared up. I never wanted him to see me doing that, but it made me emotional.

As grateful as I was to Michelle, I can't say that everything changed overnight, or that I never reverted to bad habits. I sometimes did. I struggled a lot with going back to my neighborhood and my old ways. I had lived a certain way all my life. For all the problems, that was the life I knew and was comfortable with. It's hard to break bad habits. Sometimes I fought the discipline that Michelle was trying to instill in me. Making the bed or making sure the house was clean were new responsibilities to me. Michelle, with good reason, wanted me to check in with her if I was out late. I didn't always do that. Things like that would cause some friction. On one hand, I had a better, more stable living environment with Michelle with rules and regulations that I now understand are normal. But I didn't understand that then. The pull of my old life in my old home and neighborhood was still there. I'd have friends come over to Michelle's house without asking permission. *What's the big deal?* I figured. A couple of times, she kicked me out and said, "If you want to act like that, go be back with your mom." But that only happened a couple times. It was after the first time she kicked me out that I began to think of her as a motherly figure.

That made it awkward with my actual mom. Staying with Michelle almost felt like I was sneaking out. I sometimes came around my mom's house after school, and I figured as long as I kept doing that, my mom wouldn't really notice how much I was at Michelle's. I feared what my mom would say if I told her I wanted to move in with Michelle permanently, so I just kept it to myself. It took three and a half months for my mom to finally realize I had totally moved out.

It hurt me that it took so long for my mom to realize I was living with Michelle. As a kid, you're supposed to have two people who love you unconditionally—your parents. I didn't know my dad and never cared about that. But to realize that my mom didn't seem to notice or care that I was living elsewhere bothered me. It wasn't like she and Michelle had a conversation about it and they agreed that this living arrangement would be better for everybody. She didn't know Michelle. Despite Michelle's repeated attempts, my mom continued to show no interest in getting to know her. I was still getting to know Michelle myself. My mom could have called the police and potentially gotten Michelle in trouble for having me live with her without getting permission.

When my mom finally realized that I truly was living with Michelle, things went south quickly. She believed Michelle was trying to turn me against my family. She didn't recognize that living with Michelle was best for me at the time, that she was providing me with a safe place to stay, a roof over my head, clothes on my back, and love and support that we sometimes lacked in our household. My mom didn't appreciate all that Michelle was doing for me and was worried about what others would think of this new arrangement. Over time, my relationship with Michelle changed from mentee-mentor to child-parent. The love, support, and protection she gave me were things I felt were missing from my own mom. To me, she is my mom. That's how I refer to her. My biological mother just became "Momma" to me.

Michelle Nash:

I think the first time he called me "Ma" was when we were at Target. I think we went to get school supplies. Cardale didn't even know what Target was. He was like a kid in a candy store. He was so excited about this store. I told him to get a cart and pick up some things while I shopped. I had no idea that he'd have a cart full of junk and candy. I said, "That's not what I meant." But I went ahead and bought it anyway. We were leaving Target and he called me "Ma."

I got teary-eyed. I always wanted kids. But when I was told when I was 17 that I couldn't, that was the most devastating thing that has happened to me in my life. "Mom" is not a word I thought I would ever hear about myself. I have a lot of kids to love. But never did I think I'd hear the word "Ma" from an actual person who I was taking care of. That was huge to me. That was like God answering a prayer. It really was. Again, I got teary-eyed.

Becoming teary-eyed was common for Michelle. Her emotions are close to the surface. That was something new for me. I'd never seen adults cry. I'd never really seen adults express themselves that way. I'd tease her by calling her a crybaby. If I got good grades or got commended for doing something good, she'd cry. I was like, "What is going on?"

In that way, we were opposites. I'm sure because of my upbringing, I put up a wall around myself to avoid getting hurt. When I started living with Michelle, I was at an age when I was trying to become a young man, trying to become who I was set out to be. I needed to figure out how to develop habits that would take me places I'd never been, and I'm not just talking about football. But I was wary of getting too close to people. It's an issue I still battle. Sometimes I'm one foot in, one foot out. I'm laid-back and nonchalant. I don't show too much emotion.

Even recently, after we had a minor spat, Michelle asked me a question: Do I feel like I'm worth being loved? I said that I don't even think like that. If someone loves me, they do. If they don't, I don't care. It goes back to when I was younger and feeling like the one or two people who are supposed to love you unconditionally left me out to dry. It's an unintentional defense mechanism that I developed.

But I knew Michelle cared about me, and not because I was a football player. Still, as my high school years continued and I stayed with Michelle, it wasn't easy for me socially because I didn't want it to appear as if I'd turned my back on my mother to family and friends. My siblings were extremely supportive of my decision and loved Michelle for genuinely treating me as her son. To this day, I regard Michelle as my mom. Without her, I do not know where I'd be and how different my life would have turned out.

> *Sheena Jones, sister:*
>
> *I love Michelle because she stepped up and played a big part in my brother's life when my mom couldn't be there at the time. I can't do anything but thank God for her.*

Chapter 4

BEGINNING TO BLOSSOM

WITH MICHELLE HELPING TO STABILIZE my personal life and me starting to blossom as a football player, I began to envision a future better than what had seemed possible a few years, or even months, earlier.

I was really excited about our chances my junior season. We had an opportunity to do something that no team in Glenville's impressive history had done—win a state title. We went into that season with some of the best players in the country. Christian Bryant would go on to be a star safety at Ohio State and play in the NFL. Shane Wynn was electrifying as a receiver and all-around playmaker. He went on to a great career with the Indiana Hoosiers. We had some great linemen. V'Angelo Bentley would play for Illinois as a defensive back.

We also had a new quarterbacks coach, Scott Niedzwiecki, who had a lot of experience coaching the position. At first, I was a little bit wary of Coach Niedzwiecki. He was the first white coach I'd ever had. I was thinking, *What could a white dude know about me?* The type of person I am, I needed to have a good relationship with my coach to play well. If not, it'd be in one ear and out the other when he talked to me. When he started, it was hard for me to comprehend or accept some of his coaching because I knew he'd never been in my shoes. It's hard to concentrate on X's and O's when you're worried about whether you're going to get a meal tonight.

It wasn't just that Coach Niedzwiecki was my first white coach. I'd hardly had any white teachers—just a few in elementary school. Growing up, I didn't have any white friends. None of the people I knew well were white. It wasn't until my senior year when I was staying at Michelle's in Euclid that I had my first real exposure to white peers.

But Coach Niedzwiecki won my trust. He really helped me with more complex reads and pre-snap recognition. He could build on what I'd learned from Coach Tone. Coach Niedzwiecki really opened my mind up about how hard it is to play quarterback and how rewarding it is when you put effort into it.

As a quarterback, I had to play catch-up. Nowadays, it's common for kids to have private quarterback coaches at a young age. It wasn't when I was coming up. Hell, I had no idea I'd even be a quarterback until my freshman year. Even if I had played quarterback earlier, we couldn't have afforded to hire a personal coach.

There also wasn't the explosion of camps, especially specialized ones, like there is now. At Glenville, we went on what we called the bus tour. For about a week, we'd visit a bunch of college camps in a certain area, sometimes two in one day. We'd go to a camp, eat at Golden Corral, and then go to the next camp, sometimes getting there in the middle of it.

On one of those days when we hit two camps in one day, we visited Michigan State in Lansing and then drove to Eastern Michigan in Ypsilanti. I was starting to get attention from college programs at that point, but I wasn't a blue-chip prospect. That was clear from my treatment at Michigan State's camp. That experience left me hating

Michigan State. I call it being "fuckboyed," the way I was treated. They put me with a group of lesser quarterbacks on an adjacent field from the main one and gave me this huge lineman face-mask helmet like they'd give a freaking scrub. When I got a chance to throw, I lit it up. That got their attention. They brought me to the field with the high-priority prospects. I lit it up on that field too. One of the coaches there that day—I can't remember his name—came to Ginn Academy to visit me. We were talking, and I said to him, "Man, I'm not going to lie. I can't stand you guys." We laughed about it in a joking way, and they did offer a scholarship, but in my head, I was like, *I would never go that school.*

My dream school growing up was the one most Ohio kids had: The Ohio State University. I remember watching the 2002 Ohio State team play Miami in the BCS National Championship Game. Until then, I'd never really watched a full college football game. But that year, my Pop Warner team went 11–0, which created a little buzz in our neighborhood, and I was starting to fall in love with football. Ohio State went undefeated that year too, winning a bunch of close games, and faced the mighty Hurricanes, who'd won 34 straight games, in the champion ship game. At least 25 people gathered in our living room, screaming and cheering for the underdog Buckeyes. As the game went back and forth, I remember blurting out, "Whichever team wins, that's what school I'm going to!" Of course, as a 10-year-old, I knew nothing about what it takes to earn a scholarship at a program such as Ohio State or The U. It was just something that came out of my mouth. When Ohio State prevailed in overtime, the joy that flooded our house seemed to last for months. I knew I wanted to have that same effect on people, to bring that long-lasting joy and excitement to people just as those Buckeyes had for us. One thing was clear after that game: My team's 11–0 season was no longer the buzz in our community, and rightfully so.

Ohio State might have been my dream school, but my first impressions when I attended their camp reminded me a little of when I went to Michigan State's. I wasn't one of those prospects they were giving individual attention to. I was just another guy on the outside field. I could see coaches pulling the top players inside the Woody Hayes Athletic Center for a closer work. So I snuck inside the Woody. "Hey, where's the restroom?" I asked someone as an excuse to get closer to the real action. I saw other quarterbacks doing a drill, and that's when I made my move. I jumped into the line like I belonged there. Somehow I didn't get thrown out, and I threw well. I don't know if that's when they first started to recognize me, but suddenly I was clearly on the Buckeyes' radar.

My junior season got off to a bumpy start with a 14–13 loss to defending state champion St. Ignatius. After an easy win the next week, we had a showdown with Huber Heights Wayne and their quarterback, Braxton Miller. While I was just becoming a high school starter, Braxton already was a five-star prospect. He was the one everyone expected to be the Buckeyes' next star quarterback, and he would become exactly that. Braxton had a big arm, dazzling moves, and incredible speed as a runner.

It was obviously a huge game, and for me it was a humbling week. Labor Day was the Monday before the game. We didn't have school, of course, and I assumed that meant we wouldn't practice that day. By the time I realized we did have practice, I was late. My punishment: The coaches benched me. *You've got to be kidding*, I thought. *What the hell?* But the coaches weren't bluffing. Christian Bryant, who was primarily a defensive back, was inserted at quarterback in the game. When Wayne took a 13–0 lead, I thought for sure the coaches would decide to have a change of heart and put me in. I did get my chance in the second quarter and threw a 57-yard touchdown pass on a flea flicker as we took control of the game. *It's fucking on now*, I thought, figuring there was no way they'd take me out then. But then Coach Ginn said, "Sit your ass back down." I probably played 10 snaps that game. Fortunately for us, Christian was unbelievable. He ran for a touchdown, threw for another, returned an interception 82 yards for another score, and even kicked a 35-yard field goal. We won 57–28.

JayJay Robinson:

Cardale and Coach Ginn had a great relationship, but Cardale sometimes back then didn't like people to tell him anything. Coach Ginn was the type who was going to tell you what you didn't want to hear but what you needed to hear. They would always bump heads. Coach Ginn would always try to tell us what was right and to do the right things, but sometimes as kids we just didn't want to hear it. Cardale had that fuck-it attitude, and you couldn't be that way with Coach Ginn; that was going to start a big commotion. The coach is always going to win those, especially Coach Ginn.

I remember Coach Tone talked to me afterward. "I could only imagine what your demeanor and your attitude would have been if we'd lost that game, because you'd have felt we needed you," he said. "It's bigger than you." At least I didn't have to worry about a quarterback controversy. Christian's one night of glory at that position was enough for him. Thank God for that. I remember him talking to me too. He was like, "I don't want to have to play quarterback. C'mon, dude. Get your shit together."

I did. We won the rest of our games, mostly by blowouts. We became the first Cleveland public school team to win a playoff game, which included a 30–13 revenge win over St. Ignatius. In the state semifinals, we beat Massillon Washington, which featured wide receiver Devin Smith, my future OSU teammate. I played really well that game, and we won 31–17. I threw for two touchdowns and almost 200 yards and ran for a crucial 26-yard score. I got hit as I crossed into the end zone and flipped and fell on my hip. I was in excruciating pain. Our trainer, Ace, came out. I don't know how old Ace was, but he was one of those guys who had *always* been old. He carried a gun, carried a knife, carried brass knuckles, and he chewed tobacco. He got down right in front of my face and said, "Get your bitch ass up! I'll have one of these girls rub that pussy on you if you get up." I was like, "What?" I was crying. I'll tell you this: I will never forget the smell of that chewing tobacco so close to my face.

It turned out that I was fine and played the rest of the game with no problem. I was in complete command that day. In addition to my throws and runs, I was able to show more subtle things that proved how much I'd matured as a quarterback. One time, an incorrect play call came in and the guys were all confused, and I was able to get everyone settled and in the right position. Late in the game when we were trying to milk the lead, I made sure I stayed inbounds on a run to keep the clock running.

OSU's then–head coach Jim Tressel and then–Buckeyes quarterbacks coach Nick Siciliano came to that game, and Coach Ginn told me afterward that Coach Tressel had offered me a scholarship. Coach Ginn said that Tressel really believed I was going to win a national championship at Ohio State. The dream I'd had as a boy was now becoming within reach.

That victory over Massillon sent us to the Division I state title game. If we'd won the championship, we might have been crowned the unofficial national champion. But we lost a heartbreaker to Hilliard Davidson 16–15 at Fawcett Stadium in Canton. Davidson won after they scored on a two-point conversion after a touchdown with one minute to play. I still tell people that's the best game I ever played, which made losing even harder. I think that was the first time I really ever bought in to doing all the little things the coaches preached. I remember preparing for that game and all the hype around our team and the city because we'd never won a state championship game. Every time around that time of year in the playoffs, especially if you won one or two big games, there was conversation about which was the best team to ever come through your school. We started to have those conversations, and they were legit, because no one else had made it as far as us.

We should have won that game. It's funny, but I remember details about that game and some others in high school more than I do my college games. I thought we were going to crush Hilliard Davidson. But we were undisciplined, and we also got cheated by the refs. There's no rule in the rule book where you can take a touchdown off the board after you score. But that's what happened to us in that game. I threw a 99-yard touchdown pass, a play-action bomb, to my buddy Shane Wynn. We were jogging down the field, and one of our linemen shoved one of their players. A late hit. The refs saw it and threw a flag. They took the touchdown off the board. They didn't even know where to spot the ball. The penalty was supposed to be applied on the kickoff or extra point. Complete horse crap. But we still had plenty of opportunities to win the game. But our defense missed tackles, and we dropped a lot of passes—three in the end zone. We had a fourth-and-1 that could have iced the win. We called a play we'd worked on all week. It was a fake fullback dive that we threw to a lineman. He was open, as we expected, but dropped the pass.

Ted Ginn Sr.

That was a great team. Cardale played well. We didn't lose because of him. But the discipline part of the team always comes back to get you when you need it the most.

In the locker room, we were devastated, just devastated. We were a really close team. Probably 80 percent of the players were from my neighborhood, and we knew the rest from playing with or against each other from Pop Warner on up. The seniors were so heartbroken. They were crying and saying how much they loved the team. It was tough. I was just in shock the whole time, like, no way that had just happened after the season we had, the players we had, and how hard we'd played.

Sheena Jones:

Even though Glenville lost, they had a parade for the team. They came down 123rd right past the football field and went on around to the school. A lot of the players were standing on the back of pickup trucks. Everybody was standing on both sides of the street taking pictures and waving. The churches put signs up. The store owners had pictures and news articles posted in their stores. Everybody was just proud of them.

I hoped we'd have another chance for a state title my senior year. We knew St. Edward was going to be really good. We thought in the state championship game that we might play Braxton Miller's Huber Heights Wayne team again, and I really wanted a chance for that after not playing much in our game as a junior.

But there was adversity from the start of the season. Coach Niedzwiecki had gone to another school and was replaced by a quarterbacks coach I didn't have the same rapport with. But Coach Tone had been promoted to become the play caller, and I was excited about that. Tone was my guy. He was closer to our age, and he was just a cool guy. But he was going through some issues with his day job. I can't remember exactly what they were, but he couldn't coach us for the first eight games of the season. Shane Wynn, Nick Davis—a receiver whose nickname was T.O.—and I decided that our motto would be, "Do it for Tone." I don't think that went over well with Coach Ginn, because Coach Ginn and Coach Tone had a huge falling out. I'm not sure exactly what happened with that.

Then Coach Ginn and I got into it one day during the summer. It was at a practice, and the defense was on the field. Shane and I were the only players who didn't play defense at all. Usually in that situation, I'd throw routes to a couple of receivers. But there was no room on the field for us to do it that day, so we sat on the bench and shot the shit while everyone else was practicing. Looking back on it, it did look bad. You can't be sitting down during practice like that. Coach Ginn also coached track, and those responsibilities prevented him from being present at the start of football practice that day. So when he got there, he saw us just sitting down, and he clearly wasn't happy. I think Shane got up and started walking toward the defensive backs. As Coach Ginn walked toward me, he said, "Hey, man, if you don't want to be here . . ." I got up and started looking for a place to go, and as he got to me, he kind of shoved me back over to the bench. One thing about me is I don't like public embarrassment. Even though it was only a summer practice, we had parents and fans watching. I was like, *Fuck this. I'm not gonna be all embarrassed.* So I took off my shoulder pads and threw them and walked out of practice. I went back to my neighborhood and just hung out with friends. The story spread quickly, and everybody was calling. Michelle was calling. My mom was calling. Michelle heard that Coach Ginn had put his hands on me. She had that home day care I mentioned, so she loaded up the kids and drove over to the field looking for Coach Ginn. She was seeing red; she was ready to kill him. But the falling out lasted only a day or two. Shane and I apologized to the team, and we put it behind us.

With Coach Tone absent, Coach Ginn called the plays in our first three games. It was hilarious because he hadn't done that for a long time. It was like he was trying to sneak in the signals. But we won our first three big nonconference games, including close wins over Indianapolis Warren Central and Dwyer from Palm Beach Gardens, Florida. As expected, we breezed through league play and then beat Warren Harding 41–6 in our first playoff game as the top-ranked team in the state.

That set up a regional semifinal showdown with St. Edward, which was also undefeated. We led 16–14 at halftime, but we fell apart in the second half and lost 42–22. I threw four interceptions and felt as if I had let the guys down. We would not win a state title in my last chance to win one.

As for my decision about college, in the end it wasn't close, though I didn't announce I'd be going to Ohio State until signing day in February. One of the biggest reasons I signed with Ohio State was Coach Tressel. A number of Glenville players played for him at Ohio State. Troy Smith went from an under-the-radar player to the 2006 Heisman Trophy winner. At the start of the recruiting process, we heard that Coach Tressel was a person who cared about you as a person and not just a football player. We heard he really cared about your family and was the kind of coach you'd have a relationship with forever. When I finally got a chance to get to know him, that was the truth. He rarely talked about the great things we were going to do as football players at Ohio State. It was all about life and the opportunities that football can present you, the doors it can open. When I talk now with recruits or when other people ask me, that's what I talk about. I don't need to talk about the things everyone sees. I talk about the brand and what it can do for you if you put yourself in the right position, and that's what Coach Tressel talked a lot about.

Still, I treated my recruitment like a business decision. I loved Ohio State and Coach Tressel, but I had to do my due diligence to make the right decision for me, on and off the field. I knew I'd have a better chance to play early at other places. Braxton Miller, who'd already committed to Ohio State, was the clear favorite to succeed Terrelle Pryor at quarterback. Braxton was ranked as the 29th overall prospect and the second-ranked dual-threat quarterback in the 247Sports composite rankings. I was only a three-star prospect at No. 398 and No. 10 among pro-style quarterbacks. That didn't necessarily scare me off. I wasn't afraid of competition. Troy Smith was overshadowed by Justin Zwick as a high school prospect, and look what happened with them. But it was something I had to weigh. My choices came down to OSU, Penn State, The U, and LSU.

As signing day approached, the stress started getting to me. It wasn't just that I was making such a big decision. Now that the lights, camera, and action of signing day was near, my momma wanted to be a part of it. By this time, I was fully living with Michelle. Even though she never became my legal guardian, unofficially she was. At homecoming my senior year, I hid in the locker room instead of being escorted onto the field by my momma because to do so would have been a slap in the face to Michelle. I just didn't want to fake it in front of everybody that the relationship I had with my momma was like most of the players had with their mothers. Looking back on it, do I regret it? I do. Because I made my momma cry, which wasn't a good feeling. But I didn't want to feel like a pawn. Word had started to get around that I didn't live with my momma anymore and I was living with some lady. And my momma was making up rumors about our relationship and stuff like that, spreading the idea that I didn't care about my family. I looked at all that as her attempt to engage with me and trying to show that, "Look, we're still cool. This is my son. Oh, I'm so proud of him."

We had arguments about who was going to sit with me when I signed my letter of intent. I got so pissed that one day I threw my cell phone against the wall and broke it. As my parent, my momma did have to physically sign my papers. After we both signed, she asked, "OK, what school are you going to?"—like she hadn't even paid attention to the papers we'd just signed. It was like she didn't care which school. *You'll just sign me over to anything, huh?* I thought.

Though I signed with Ohio State, there was a catch. During one of my unofficial visits to Columbus, I met with Coach Siciliano, director of football operations Greg Gillum, and director of player development Stan Jefferson about delaying my arrival. OSU coaches didn't want Braxton and me to enter Ohio State at the same time. They wanted some separation between us, so they suggested I delay my enrollment at Ohio State. They'd talked with Coach Ginn, and all of them had a place in mind. "OK, cool. I'll do it," I said.

In what would become a recurring theme, I didn't know what I was getting myself into.

Chapter 5

PIT STOP

I PROBABLY SHOULD HAVE LOOKED UP Fork Union's complete name before I got there. When Ohio State coaches suggested the Virginia school, they described it as a prep school. I never bothered to Google it. If I had, I'd have learned its full name. Instead, I found out the hard way. Even getting there to enroll was a challenge. My brother Jay, Sheena, and my momma drove with me. The plan was to sleep the night before at my family's home, but my brother and I couldn't sleep because the bed had bedbugs. We were supposed to leave in the morning but didn't leave until about 3:00 or 4:00 the next afternoon. We barely got there before orientation started.

> *Jay Jones:*
>
> *I remember getting there like right in the nick of time because everything was put on me to get him there, and I want to say that we didn't have the money. I can't remember the details. I can't remember what we drove. But it wasn't getting just gas money; I had to get my mother together because she needed to be*

> *there to sign papers. Oh, and we needed to eat and we needed hotel money.*
>
> *I didn't know how he was getting there until like the week of. There were a lot of moving parts to put together in a short amount of time. I remember reaching out to my family: "Hey, do y'all have anything to help pay for this trip? Because I don't have it by myself."*

When we arrived, we were told to go to all these different stations to check in. I was walking around and seeing all these people in uniforms, and I was just looking at them, confused. I had a bag with my own clothes. A guy said, "Oh, you don't need clothes like that here. You wear these uniforms every day." I remember walking to the chapel hall for orientation and seeing guys with their shirts tucked into their shorts. I was like, *What the fuck's wrong with that guy?* Then I noticed something else, or I should say the absence of something else. *Where the fuck are the girls?* I walked into orientation and realized there weren't any. Then I saw the sign behind me: FORK UNION MILITARY ACADEMY. Finally, it hit me. I thought, *What is going on right now?* The school's dean started talking about Fork Union's rules. It felt like I was having a bad dream. "Where am I? I'm leaving right now. Don't leave me here," I said. Then the dean told the families to say goodbye, that it was time for their sons to start to get adjusted. At least I had my cell phone. That at least could be a link to the outside world. Then the dean said cell phones weren't allowed.

My first or second night there, I remember crying. We were told to write letters home and could only watch TV during limited times. I was like, *What the fuck is going on? I didn't intend to sign up for this.* I was just there to kill time before enrolling at Ohio State. Now I had to live like a soldier?

Ted Ginn Sr.

That's probably the only decision that was made for him that he probably didn't agree to. Tress and I tricked him. But it was for his protection. He got another year to mature and play. He was not going to go down to OSU with Braxton and be with two or three other quarterbacks and sit on the bench. He wasn't mature enough for that. So Tress and I felt that him going to Fork Union would help him. I think it did.

I wasn't the only future OSU player at Fork Union. Wide receiver Mike Thomas also was there, I think because he was young for his grade and his parents wanted him to experience being in a highly structured environment, almost serving as a gap before he came all the way from Los Angeles to Columbus. Though we roomed together, we weren't particularly close at Fork Union. We kind of had an understanding that we'd just get through this shit separately and then form happier memories at Ohio State. But I could tell he was feeling the same way about Fork Union as I was. He was sitting behind me in class one day and I could hear him sniffling back tears. I was like, *We're both in here crying like a motherfucker*. Sometimes it felt more like a prison than a school. A lot of the rules and regulations didn't make sense to us.

People went to Fork Union for a lot of reasons. Some planned to go into the military, and this was good training. Some were sent because of disciplinary or maturity issues. Others went to try to earn athletic scholarship offers. Fork Union had both high school and postgraduate football teams. The high school team was quarterbacked by Christian Hackenberg, who'd go on to play at Penn State. I was on the postgraduate team, but as someone who already had committed to school, I was mostly a backup to a guy, Mike Fafaul, who was continuing the recruiting process because he was looking for a big-time scholarship offer out of high school. Fafaul would go to UCLA as a preferred walk-on before eventually starting late in his Bruins career. The guys who were already committed usually only played when we were down or the starters were struggling. I played significant time, though, maybe 40 percent of the snaps.

I won't say that I got nothing out of Fork Union. I bonded with a few guys and still talk to some to this day. My time there did help me become more self-disciplined. You had to do things when no one was watching, like always keeping your shoes shined, your uniform up to spec, your room clean. The first extended break I got after I enrolled in late August was at Thanksgiving. I went home, and it was great seeing everyone in Cleveland. It also made returning to Fork Union even harder, though I had to go back for only two and a half weeks before the semester was over. I got dropped off at the airport wearing my uniform, called Class As, and didn't bother to tuck in my shirt. I was also holding my hat in my hands. A man who was in the military approached me. "Hey, sir. Can I speak to you for a second?" he said. He asked where I was going, and I told him. Then he lit into me: "If you don't fucking take your ass into the bathroom right now and fix your uniform . . ." At that point, I think I mentally blacked out because I was so nervous and scared.

Honestly, my time at Fork Union also taught me to be sneaky. Being that age and not having a cell phone was almost impossible. I managed to find a way to sneak a phone in. I had an earpiece and hid the phone in what we called the boot blouse in the bottom of our fatigues, so it wasn't visible. Finally, in December my semester at Fork Union was up. I couldn't wait to leave. When I'd been in Cleveland, I grabbed some casual clothes like sweatpants because I did not want to bring any of my Fork Union military clothes back to Cleveland with me. On my final day, I gave some school-issued stuff, such as my shoeshine kit, to other students. The rest I left in my room. I wanted no reminders of the place. Literally as soon as I put one foot off campus, I changed into sweats and dumped my Class A uniform in the trash. It was the best feeling in the world. Such a relief. *I'm out of here, and I'm never coming back*, I thought.

I was so happy to be headed to Columbus to start my college career after this detour. But I would be playing for a different Ohio State coaching staff than I expected to when I signed my letter of intent in February 2011. In the spring of my senior year of high school, OSU's tattoo and memorabilia scandal broke. Several star players, including quarterback Terrelle Pryor, had received benefits that were in violation of NCAA rules at the time. Worse, Coach Tressel signed an NCAA form claiming he had no knowledge of it, though it came out later that he did. Memorial Day weekend, he was fired, and Luke Fickell was named interim coach.

By Ohio State standards, the 2011 season was a disaster. Pryor left school, and the other players involved were suspended for several games. Braxton Miller was forced into action before he was probably ready. Ohio State lost its last four games to finish 6–7, with a losing record for the first time since 1988. Right after the Michigan game, Ohio State hired Urban Meyer as its head football coach. Right away, I was concerned because I wasn't sure his spread offense would be a good fit for my skill set. I knew he liked quarterbacks who could run as well as pass. Yes, I could run, but I was no Braxton. I thought I'd never get a chance to play there. As a Fork Union student, other schools were allowed to recruit me, even though I was bound for Ohio State. And they did, telling me all the things I suspected they would about me not being a fit for Meyer's system. Every time a new OSU offensive coach was hired to Coach Meyer's staff, I researched his background, the type of quarterbacks used and the style of offense. I was looking for anything and everything I could to ease my mind about going to Ohio State.

Meyer's new offensive coordinator and quarterbacks coach was Tom Herman, who came from Iowa State. He came to visit me at Fork Union. What would normally be a two-year process of developing a relationship, we tried to cram into a one-hour meeting. I found Coach Herman to be a straight shooter.

> *Tom Herman:*
>
> *I'd been told Cardale was an extremely physically talented player with tremendous upside. Huge frame, strong arm, and he could extend plays with his athletic ability.*
>
> *Cardale was a very respectful young man. I could tell he wanted to learn and was eager to develop. He had a gregarious personality and was easy to get along with.*

During Coach Herman's visit, he asked me for my cell number so he could reach me. Because cell phones were against regulations, I lied and told him I didn't have one, and gave him my email to use to contact me. He didn't really believe me. He figured students would find a way to get phones. But I insisted. I'd just met him; I wasn't going to trust him. I didn't know if he would snitch on me. So I knew I was lying, and he probably thought I was lying. That was how our relationship started.

> *Tom Herman:*
>
> *It was actually a great icebreaker. I think that once I told him that there was no way he didn't have a phone stashed somewhere, he understood that I could relate to him and he could trust me. He was worried that I would rat him out, and I made sure to let him know*

that I had his best interests in mind and I just wanted a way to get ahold of him so that we could just start building our relationship over the phone.

Coach Herman told me Ohio State would still honor my scholarship and that the coaching staff was excited about my ability and what I could bring to the offense. He told me hard work and leadership were requirements in the quarterback room.

The meeting reassured me about my decision to attend Ohio State. But I would find out very quickly how different Coach Meyer was from Coach Tressel.

Chapter 6

BUMPY START AT OHIO STATE

I WAS EXCITED TO MEET Urban Meyer. I knew what he had done at Florida, winning two national championships. The second came in 2006 with a stunning 41–14 upset of No. 1 Ohio State that featured Glenville's Troy Smith and Ted Ginn Jr.

I had about two and a half weeks at home in Cleveland after leaving Fork Union before winter quarter started at Ohio State. I was still in Cleveland when the Buckeyes finished their season with a loss to Florida in the Gator Bowl on a Sunday. On Monday we had a team meeting at the Woody Hayes Athletic Center with Coach Meyer before classes started later that day. I had just arrived in Columbus when we had our introduction to Coach Meyer. He had been on the job for a month, but Coach Fickell and the old staff coached the Gator Bowl while Meyer assembled his staff and got settled. So this was really his first meeting with the returning players. I showed up for the meeting still carrying my bags and stuff from home with me.

I assumed Coach Meyer would be as excited to meet us as we were to meet him. He had grown up in Ashtabula in far northeastern Ohio as a huge Buckeyes fan. He started his career as a grad assistant at Ohio State after graduating from the University of Cincinnati. Now he'd come full circle and was back in his home state taking over one of the best programs in college football. You'd never have known that from his first meeting. He acted as if he had inherited a terrible program. He raised his voice and was clearly unimpressed with us. It didn't help that several veteran players showed up late. They'd just gotten back from the Gator Bowl the night before and had obviously overslept. Coach Meyer talked about the proud tradition of Ohio State and how the 2011 team hadn't lived up to it. "You guys suck, and there's going to be a lot of changes," he said. He even said that he'd heard things about players being on drugs and doing other things they shouldn't.

I'd come into the meeting starstruck because of what Coach Meyer had done at Florida and the anticipation of what he'd do at Ohio State. This was not the Urban Meyer I had been expecting. I was like, *What is going on?* Then Mickey Marotti, the head strength coach and Coach Meyer's right-hand man, got up in front of the team and started talking. This wasn't a good cop, bad cop deal; this was a bad cop, bad cop deal. "You guys aren't shit!" Marotti—who we called Coach Mick—yelled. "You're soft. You're not tough. I moved my family across the country for this. My daughter has been to four different high schools in four years, and she's tougher than you guys." Coach Mick then announced that workouts—Attitude Training, he called it—would start the next day at 5:45 AM, and he walked out, like *Screw you guys*. His message was clear: *Your asses are mine.*

All this was stunning to me. Here I was, just getting to Ohio State after spending a semester at a military school that I didn't really want to attend. I had no part in the bad 2011 season. And yet the new freshmen were being put in the same boat as the veterans. I sat in the back of the room during the meeting. After Coach Meyer and Coach Mick left, fullback Zach Boren asked the players to stay for a minute. Boren raised his voice in defiance. "We're not going to let these new coaches come here and treat us like that," he said. "We're going to show them. We're going to bust our butts this off-season."

Not everyone was on board. Running back Carlos Hyde got up and said, "Man, I'm not trying to hear that shit." He started to walk out. Zach yelled back, "Carlos, that's what the hell I'm talking about!" and they just started fighting in front of the whole team. This was my first experience in college. I was just watching this in disbelief.

That wasn't the only way my Ohio State experience got off to a disorienting start. For some reason, they didn't have a spot for me in the athletic dorm where the other young players lived. I got placed with three nonathletes in a regular dorm. That was super awkward. The dorm, Nosker House, was on Woodruff Avenue. It was about a 35-minute walk along Lane Avenue and then across the bridge over the Olentangy River to the Woody, but in those early days, I hadn't figured out how to get there. I didn't even know the street names at that point. I think it took me two hours to find it the first day.

I woke up about 3:30 in the morning and got to the Woody by 5:45. I got there and all the players were in the parking lot. When they tried to use their key fobs to enter the Woody, they didn't work. Everyone was trying to figure out what was going on when the strength coaches came walking by. They told us that we'd have to work out outside—no locker room access for us. Snow was on the ground, and it felt like it was freaking 10 degrees. Everyone was talking: "What the fuck is going on? They're trippin'. Why aren't we inside? We have an indoor facility. Blah, blah, blah." Then the coaches lined us up five or six deep on one of the outside fields. We were doing jumping jacks, push-ups, and body squats. Then we were sent to the end zone and had to do bear crawls the length of the whole field and back.

What are bear crawls? You're on all fours, can't have your knees touch the ground, and you crawl like a bear. Literally, your hands and feet are moving at the same time and you're crawling 100 yards and back. Then we had to do bear crawls using only one leg. Remember, there was snow on the ground. The turf was frozen, so our hands were frozen as well. Oh, and I should add that we weren't allowed to wear any Ohio State gear. We hadn't earned that privilege, we were told. We were wearing whatever we had on when we got there. And because I'd already had that long way just to get to the Woody because I didn't know how to get there, I was already tired and a little sweaty by the time I arrived.

After the bear crawls, we had to do lunges, again 100 yards and back. If you stopped or put your feet together, you had to start over. Then we'd do these things called barrel walks. We'd pair up with a teammate. One of us would hold the other player's legs while he "walked" using only his arms for 50 yards. Then we would switch roles for the 50 yards back. I got paired with Andrew Norwell, a 330-pound offensive lineman. You wanted to be with someone your size because if you were struggling to hold the other player's legs, it was harder for him to use his arms to walk. Clearly, it was easier for him to carry me than me to carry him because he was a lot heavier than I was. I was struggling. My arms were already dead from holding his legs, so it was hard. I remember him yelling at me, "Freaking hold my legs!" I thought he was about to kill me.

For other drills, we'd divide into three groups. One group would be on a pull-ups and dips bar. I remember one day I was paired up with Storm Klein, a linebacker, and I was looking down at the concrete and was like, *I'm about to let go and let my face hit the concrete because I can't take this anymore*. He was holding my legs and cheering, "You got it, man! You got it! Just hold on!" Another group would be doing squats and push-ups and jumping jacks. Another group would be doing sled pushes, another grueling drill. When we were done, we'd be told abruptly, "Get out. Same time tomorrow." No showers. No access to the locker room. Just go to class and repeat the same thing the next day. I remember walking around campus using a map to find my way to my classes, and I was in the most pain of my life. I was taking the smallest steps possible because of the pain I was in. I was thinking that I didn't know if I wanted to go back to that the next day. I thought then, and still do, that the coaches were making stuff up on the fly just to see who would give up. Many guys did quit. They decided to transfer before we ever really got far into our off-season program. It was insane. Guys who had playing experience just decided, *No, we ain't doing this. We ain't putting up with this.*

Tyvis Powell, early-enrollee freshman:

Hell. That's what it was like: hell.

I remember calling Coach Ginn and asking if it was too late to go to another school to play the 2012 season. Back then, you had to sit out a year if you transferred. I don't think Coach Ginn gave me an answer, because he didn't want me to give up and transfer before spring practice had even started. But I was like, "These dudes are crazy here, and they don't like us. I keep getting punished for something I didn't do." They kept talking about the players who sold memorabilia. I didn't do that shit. I'm convinced the coaches probably had no clue who I was, anyway. One coach I did know, Taver Johnson, was the lead guy in my recruitment. He was only on the staff for a few days while I was there before he took a job at Arkansas. During my recruitment, I thought he was the nicest guy in the world. But when I got to Ohio State, I remember him being completely different as a coach, yelling at me. When he left, I literally knew no one else on the staff. I knew

Luke Fickell was there (he stayed on under Meyer) but I didn't know him.

What made it even harder was that I was kind of in between recruiting classes. Technically I was in the 2011 class. But those guys spent that year together, as hard as it was, and had formed their friendships. I arrived in January 2012 but didn't know the players in the 2012 class. They all had a chance to bond with each other. I felt like I was there literally alone, especially since I lived in that dorm far apart from my teammates. The few times I did hang out with those guys, I had that long walk home, which sucked. The few older guys who played in high school with me, such as Christian Bryant, lived off campus. My only time with my teammates was when we were getting crushed during workouts. Since we weren't allowed in the locker room, I missed out on that opportunity to build camaraderie with them in there.

I wasn't sure I was going to survive those early conditioning workouts. In the weight room, the freshmen did their workouts at 6:00 AM, earlier than the older players. There were only about eight or nine of us, which meant that we didn't get any real break between drills. I'd never really done workouts that were that intense before, and it showed. At Glenville, we lacked the resources to have a bona fide weight room and year-round strength program.

Because I had that long walk from Nosker House, I usually didn't eat breakfast. No places were even open where I could get food. Back then, NCAA rules didn't allow programs to feed their players anything more than snacks. Trying to do those drills on an empty stomach left me feeling like I was going to die.

I somehow made it through the winter workouts but got in trouble at the start of spring practice. I was in Cleveland the weekend before spring ball started, and the Greyhound bus that brought me back to Columbus was delayed. I was late for the first team meeting of the spring. My punishment was something called Dawn Patrol at 5:45 in the morning. That included completing 200 flights on the StairMaster in 30 minutes. If you didn't, you had to do 30 more minutes. They called it doing the Empire State Building because that's about how many steps it was. What made me look even worse was that Mike Vrabel, the former New England Patriot who'd become an assistant coach for us the previous year, would do that just for fun. He'd already be on the StairMaster for probably 20 minutes and was doing it with ease. I looked over at him, thinking, *You've got to be kidding. This dude's an animal.*

I remember lying one day to Kenny Parker, one of our strength coaches, about completing the StairMaster. He'd set the intervals in a way that would allow you to get to 200 flights in 30 minutes if you kept a certain pace. It was pretty much on for 25 seconds and then off for the next 35, but you were still moving enough to keep pace. But I switched the pace to a slower one and didn't know the machine would show that the pace had been slowed. Coach Parker came to check on me at the 30-minute mark, and I was like at 180 flights. He asked if I'd switched the pace and I muttered that I hadn't. He said, "You're lying to my face." So we started off on a bad foot, and for the whole next year, he'd give me mean looks and treat me like he didn't trust me.

My first real interaction with Coach Meyer wasn't good either. The morning after I was assigned Dawn Patrol, I finished that workout and was alone in the locker room as I got ready to shower. I started playing my music. Let's just say it wasn't G-rated. As I got out of the shower, I saw that Coach Meyer had walked into the locker room. "Is this your music?" he asked me. I told him it was. He then told me how inappropriate it was. "What if my family was here?" he said. "What if someone's wife was here and was walking around this locker room and heard this dirty language? Turn it off."

I'd been at Ohio State for three months, and this was my first one-on-one experience with Coach Meyer. When he thought of me, he thought of me playing dirty music and thought I was a dirty-ho guy. Just another you've-got-to-be-kidding-me moment.

But wait, it gets worse. I don't think I got a rep until the third day of spring practice. Braxton, his backup Kenny Guiton, and walk-on Justin Siems got snaps while I just watched. On the third day, Coach Herman told me in our quarterbacks meeting that he'd give me the last rep of the final seven-on-seven drill against the starting defense. I still remember the play: Trey Right 60 Under. I'd throw an out pattern to the backside receiver cutting to the sideline. Coach Herman had explained the play's concept, and I knew exactly what to do. I waited all practice for my coming-out moment. *Now I'm going to show everyone what I can do*, I thought. *Oh, yeah, this is it. This is my chance to show everyone what I can do.* I took the snap and saw the defense was rolling to a high Cover-1 structure. The receiver, T. Y. Williams, ran his pattern as he was supposed to. In my head, I was like, *I know my read. I've got this.* In my imagination, this was the start of my rise. Sure, I wasn't recruited by this coaching staff, but here would be the first pass in an Ohio State uniform on what I hoped would eventually lead to a Heisman Trophy and status among the greatest OSU quarterbacks ever.

But my nerves got the better of my brain. I panicked. Everything happened so fast—too fast. Instead of taking the proper three-step drop, I took five. Or maybe it was seven. I kept backing up and backing up before planting my feet. Then I hitched. That threw off the timing even more. I was super late. T. Y. was probably out of bounds by the time I threw the ball. The throw sailed on me and went super high. I remember Christian Bryant laughing and screaming, "You're a bum! You're a bum!" I was used to this from high school when we'd rip each other in fun. But this wasn't Glenville. This was my first chance to make an impression at Ohio State, and I was completely embarrassed. I had just screwed up my only chance to potentially play there or show I knew what I was doing. Urban said to Tom Herman with disbelief, "What are we doing? What was that? Is that what we're teaching?" I could feel Coach Meyer's eyes burning a hole through the back of my head with disbelief at that horrible throw. But I couldn't let what Coach Meyer said go unchallenged. I was already embarrassed by the throw, and I didn't appreciate him embarrassing me even more. Other players made bad plays without being humiliated publicly. I wasn't going to take that from anybody, even Coach Meyer. "I don't know who the fuck you're talking to," I said. "I'm here for a reason." My outward bravado aside, that was a low moment. I jogged off the field in shame, thinking, *I'll never play here. I'm done.* Everyone knew I was already in the doghouse with Dawn Patrol every day, and now they thought I couldn't even play.

J. T. Barrett, OSU quarterback:

I wasn't there yet, but he's told me the story. I think that comes from him growing up in Cleveland. The guys from Glenville, that's just a rough life growing up where they're from. You grow up tougher. If you say something to somebody and they take it as disrespect, then there's something that has to be done. A lot of people don't grow up like that. They'd be like, Oh, those are just words. If you hit me, that's assault, right? *Nah. That's something that gets handled up there in Cleveland. If you said something I don't like, I'm going to say something about it. I think it's crazy how they grew up, because of how rough that was. But also, that's just a normal exchange. That's just how Cardale was.*

It didn't get better the rest of spring practice. In the spring game, when it's traditional for even the lowliest walk-on to play, I didn't get one rep. I was ready to transfer. I thought back to Coach Herman's visit at Fork Union. At the time, I figured it was because I was genuinely wanted at Ohio State. Why else would he visit? But after my first winter and spring, I started to think differently. He probably visited only because OSU needed another body at quarterback and didn't want to have to try to recruit another one with everything else he had on his plate. But after the start I'd had, it was hard for me to see how things could end well for me at Ohio State.

> *Tom Herman:*
>
> *I don't think Cardale truly understood early in his career the discipline and focus in everything in life that is needed to succeed at quarterback at a place like Ohio State. His on-the-field performance was never an issue. He loves football with all of his heart, and that was evident to me from the beginning. Cardale is a fun-loving young man with an infectious personality, and taking the job of quarterback seriously 100 percent of the time was a learning process for him, and he developed those skills over time. He's a bit of a class clown, which I can relate to, so he had to learn when it was time to have fun and when it was time to lock in and work.*

In the summer, players worked out on their own. NCAA rules at the time prevented coaches from doing any on-field work with us. Any football-related activities were led by the leaders of each position group. It was a critical time for team-building and establishing accountability. But I didn't take advantage of it. After the winter and spring I'd had, I was completely discouraged about my football prospects at Ohio State. I would show up late or not come at all. *Why waste my time?* I thought. I needed hands-on coaching from coaches, not players. I figured I'd fly under the radar until I finally got my chance to play, if it ever came. Hell, I'd been on campus for six months and wasn't sure if the coaches even knew my name.

My struggles continued in training camp. Even the way I grip the ball became an issue, though I admit it is quite unusual. I usually don't put my fingers on the laces. I started doing that when I was a raw quarterback at Glenville. Coach Ginn wanted me to speed up my motion and developed a drill to help me. He'd empty his ball bag and toss me a ball. As soon as I'd throw, he'd toss me another, and I'd have to fire right away. In that drill, I didn't have time to find the laces. When I discovered I could throw perfectly fine without finding the laces, I kept doing it that way.

In camp, we did a drill throwing deep balls. Coach Meyer noticed me throwing without the laces. "Tom, we just had a quarterback throw a go route with no laces," he said to Herman. "What are we doing?" It didn't matter that the ball was on target. Just the idea of a quarterback throwing without laces seemed inconceivable to them. Coach Herman tried quite a bit to get me to use laces, but to this day I prefer not to.

Chapter 7

THE TWEET

OK, I KNOW YOU'VE BEEN waiting for this.

The Tweet.

You probably remember what I said: "Why should we have to go to class if we came here to play FOOTBALL, we ain't come to play SCHOOL, classes are POINTLESS."

As soon as I sent it, I was branded as just another dumb athlete who didn't care about academics. Let me give you some background and clear up some misconceptions.

The irony is that at the time I posted that tweet, academics were my priority at Ohio State. After the winter and spring I'd had with the football team, I had concluded that my best chance to excel at Ohio State was in the classroom. I'd always been a pretty good student. Though the Cleveland public schools didn't really push me hard academically, I did well, especially in math and social studies. In the subjects that didn't come as easily, I tried extra hard to do as well as possible. When I started at the Ginn Academy, we had a teacher, Miss Thornton—better known as Miss T—who explained to us in depth just what society thought of young Black men, or more precisely, how *little* society thought of young Black men. My mom, an uncle, or a coach might have preached about academics, but it just hit different the way Miss T broke it down to us. She was a really good teacher. Everybody loved her. She was just real. She'd cuss you out if it was needed. She'd tell you how it was.

But she was also really good at relating to us. To graduate, we had to pass the Ohio Graduation Test. I think the proficiency rate was like 18 out of 40 or 42. That percentage would be an F in a regular class. "It's less than 50 percent," Miss T said. "That's what they think of you guys." She'd show us the requirements of other districts and other states. I remember her telling us, "They're just telling you that if you're a smart enough dummy, they'll let you out of high school." We all looked at it like it was messed up that the standard was so low. But my siblings, cousins, friends, and I took our studies seriously. We'd clown each other if we didn't do well in the classroom. I had some friends who would go to Tri-C community college for half of the day and take college classes. I wasn't on that level, but I did take academics seriously.

When I started at Ohio State, the school was still on the quarters system. I liked that because the pace was faster. You'd be introduced to new material, study it for two or two and a half weeks, and then have a midterm. Then you'd get new material and get tested again on the final exam. Classes didn't drag on. But Ohio State switched to the semester system in the fall of 2012. That was an adjustment, especially considering all the work we had to do for football.

OK, now to the tweet. It was the first week of October, and we were getting ready to play Nebraska. Both of us were undefeated. We were ranked 12th after a big 17–16 win at Michigan State the previous week. The Cornhuskers were No. 21. This was going to be a prime-time game in the Horseshoe, and there was a lot of anticipation for it. Coach Meyer talked about making it a Scarlet in the Shoe night. Not that I was going to play. I was still buried on the depth chart.

I might have been discouraged about that from a football perspective, but it made me put a bigger priority on my classes. If I couldn't succeed in football, I sure as hell was determined not to squander my opportunity academically.

We had a test in a sociology class, and I really dove hard into preparing for it, studying all week and working with tutors. I had an A in the class and wanted to keep it. I wasn't going to be satisfied with a B or C. I wanted something spectacular. If I did that, I thought it also might help my shaky standing with the coaches. It would be evidence I was maturing.

I took the test and thought I did well. When the tests were graded, I went to the auditorium where the class was and got my grade. It was a B-. I was bummed. I felt as bad as if I'd gotten an F. A teacher's assistant was the one who handed out the test results, and I wanted to talk to the TA, but so did a bunch of other students. I had another class right after that, so I couldn't wait forever. So from the back of the auditorium, in my frustration and disappointment, I typed you-know-what into my phone, hit *post*, and left for my next class.

At first, I thought nothing of my tweet. I was just a fourth-string quarterback. Who would pay attention to anything I had to say? But I'd underestimated the weight attached to anybody associated with Ohio State. As I walked up Woodruff Avenue, I saw that my phone was blowing up. Twitter was still new, and I don't think I had more than 2,000 or 3,000 followers. Facebook was the dominant social media site then. So when I saw all these likes and comments and retweets, I thought, *Cool. This is pretty sweet. I'm Twitter-famous now.*

Tyvis Powell:

I happened to be the first person to be there when he tweeted it. We were walking up the street together,

> *and he goes, "Yeah, man. I just tweeted out that, 'Yeah, we didn't come here to play school.' I looked at him and said, "You did* what*?" As I was saying that, his phone was going crazy. I was like, "Bro, you gotta go delete that. You messed up with this one. You blew it. You can't be talking like that."*
>
> When you're a quarterback at The Ohio State University, you're under a magnifying glass. Everything you do is watched because everybody is waiting for stuff like this so they can take it and run with it. I think he was thinking, *Well, I'm just a freshman, nobody big-time. Nobody will really care.*

Some people were agreeing with what I tweeted. Others didn't, and I was replying, "Fuck you. You're not in my shoes. You don't know me." Just going back and forth with people. As this was going on, I was getting calls from coaches and my academic advisor, Pierre Banks. I was ignoring them, like "Y'all gotta wait, because I'm going at it on Twitter." Coach Herman finally got through to me and said, "Dale, what's going on, on Twitter? You tweeted something or posted something?" (A lot of the guys and coaches called me Dale for short.) I said, "Yeah, I'm tweeting. What are you talking about?"

He ordered me to come to the Woody. I told him I had another class. He told me to forget that class and come to the facility immediately. I got to the Woody but had no idea this tweet was blowing up as big as it did. I saw other players there, and they were like, "Dude, what did you tweet earlier? You just tweeted that?" And they were laughing at me, like, "You're dumb as hell, but I agree with you." Like I was the stupid one for saying it publicly.

I walked into Coach Meyer's office, and he was in there with Coach Herman and, I think, athletic director Gene Smith, along with Pierre. Pierre was a former player himself. He played at Appalachian

State and was the leading tackler and recovered a fumble in the Mountaineers' famous upset of Michigan in 2007. He knew I was in deep trouble and tried to cover for me. As soon as I walked in, Pierre said, "Hey, Cardale, I was trying to tell them that you and your girlfriend just broke up and she got access to your social media and was tweeting dumb stuff from your account. Right?" But I didn't catch on that he was trying to save my ass. So I said, "No, that was me!" Like I was proud of it. He was looking at me in disbelief, with the coaches behind him, so they couldn't see his face. He was looking at me with this dead face like I had to be the dumbest motherfucker he'd ever seen in his life. The coaches told me they didn't need this type of distraction around the team right then. "Go home," they told me. "Just go back to your dorm, and don't show up for the game tomorrow."

My family was already planning to come, using the tickets we got as players. I had to call home to say that my tickets for the Nebraska game had been revoked. That sucked, because one of the few things I had to look forward to that year was giving my family tickets. My uncle, who was going to bring a buddy, still came to Columbus, and we went to Buffalo Wild Wings to watch the game, which we won 63–38 in what was a breakout game for Braxton and the OSU offense.

The next day when we met as a team, the coaches talked about how well we played and how we had to continue our momentum. I wanted to be as invisible as I could in that meeting room, but I felt like I was in the middle of everybody, in a spotlight. There was no escaping it. My tweet had been on ESPN the day of the game; they were talking about it. The Big Ten Network, they were talking about it. *Good Morning America*, they were talking about it. Every news outlet you can think of was talking about the tweet and about the perception of what college thinks, particularly at Ohio State. I wasn't speaking for anybody. I was just speaking for myself, and really was just speaking out of immaturity. I was honestly just disappointed in myself for getting a B– on that exam.

At practice after that team meeting, Coach Meyer singled me out in front of everyone, like, "Hey, I've got a freaking fourth-string or fifth-string quarterback making national headlines taking attention off the team. Don't you ever do that again. Understand?" All I could do was say, "Yes, sir." That was probably the most embarrassing moment of my college career.

> *Urban Meyer:*
>
> *I understand players probably better than most. Yeah, I have a reputation of being hard on them. But I'm also very understanding and give guys second chances probably more than anybody, so I kind of honestly laughed at it. What someone tweets, I don't care. I was more concerned that he wasn't handling his business in the classroom. I didn't know that he was upset about getting only a B on that test.*
>
> *But the stuff that comes across your desk when you're the head coach, it's nonstop. I remember actually laughing about it. The media blew it up. I certainly didn't.*

I think that's funny that something I did, especially so early in my career, amused Coach Meyer. But I agree with the way he responded at the time as a head coach coming into a program and trying to get it back on track. As an 18-year-old kid, I was scared shitless and felt his stare through the back of my skull as he ripped me in front of the team, but I now agree with the way he responded. Now knowing how he really felt, it's kind of funny that he thought it was funny.

But I was wrong to do it. That tweet was the most selfish, immature thing I'd ever done in my collegiate career—taking the spotlight away from the team and its success and bringing negative attention not just to the program and university but also to my family. My relatives had always preached the importance of doing well in school. Now I gave the impression that academics didn't matter—to me or for Ohio State athletes. The truth is that we took great pride in our overall team GPA. Our coaches stressed it. Coach Meyer started a program called Real Life Wednesdays, in which we'd meet with business leaders, get career advice, and get a step toward a post-football career.

But here's the thing: Though I shouldn't have tweeted it, I do stand behind the message of what I said. If you look at college football and college athletics in general, players aren't recruited because of their grades. Coaches and universities have to tweak the rules and do a lot to get many guys academically cleared to play. I don't remember any coach ever coming into my living room or into my high school and saying, "Hey, we have such an unbelievable marketing program at Ohio State. Fisher College is amazing. You've got to check out Fisher. I can't wait to get you into our academic program." Yeah, that's part of it, don't get me wrong. But what they're selling most are the dreams on the athletic field. We're buying the dream of playing in front of 100,000 people, which they are selling. Yeah, school is an aspect of being a student-athlete, but what drove us to that university was sports.

I think what people really reacted to was my comment that classes were pointless. I get it: it's a double-edged sword. Athletic careers aren't guaranteed. But it's also not guaranteed that a premed student is going to be a doctor. It's not guaranteed that a journalism student is going to be a successful journalist. I always thought, *Why aren't there any classes that will help me prepare to be a professional athlete? Why can't I go to a film-study quarterback class? Why can't*

I go to a class about how to manage my body? Why can't I major in my sport? People do it all the time in other professions and careers. If they don't always pan out, do you say they wasted their college career on education? No. They find something else to do, just like an athlete could do if they want to major in football or basketball or baseball. I think universities should have courses that will help them reach the career goals they choose.

> *J. T. Barrett:*
>
> *I wasn't at Ohio State yet when he tweeted that. But this is how smart Cardale is: "We don't come here to play school." How wild that he said that—and he got thrashed for it—but also how forward-thinking for his time he was. That was 2012, and they just started getting paid in 2021 with NIL stuff. These kids are not coming here to play school. Who would have said that? And he said it his way. I think that's crazy to think about it. People on the outside could argue that these kids needed some compensation for the things they do. But for a student-athlete to be in school and say that was outrageous at that time. The fact that he thought just to say it and say it just like that—"We didn't come here to play school"—that said a lot.*

I think as a society we choose when we want to choose perception and when it benefits us. Think about all the art majors out there. Think about how many good artists there are. But there are a lot fewer world-renowned artists, and even artists who can make a living from it, than there are professional athletes. Or at least I'm pretty sure it's harder to get to that level than it is in sports. For a person to say, "I want to be a famous artist" and learn everything about the history of art and culture, why can't I laugh at you the way people laugh at the idea of a college kid focused on being an athlete. You're trying to get into a field where less than 1 percent of that 1 percent of 1 percent make it.

That's what I think now. What I realized then was that I'd kept digging myself deeper and deeper into the Ohio State doghouse.

Chapter 8

STARTING TO GET IT

I DIDN'T PLAY ONE SNAP in the 2012 season. The one time I came close, I prayed I wouldn't. That kind of sums up my freshman year.

I still had a lot of growing up to do. The infamous tweet might not even have been my worst one that day. Thank God they only popped me on that one tweet, because I posted so much shit after it. "What the fuck does this class have to do with me being a better quarterback?" was one. But the one that got attention was enough.

My relationship with Coach Herman was horrible. I couldn't care less what he said or felt. He didn't like me; I didn't like him. I felt he wasn't really trying to coach me, and I wasn't listening to him anyway. There was such friction. I think he was at a point where he felt, *If this dude doesn't want to help himself, I'm done wasting my breath on him*. It's my understanding that his wife, Michelle, pushed back on him on my behalf, saying not to give up on me, which he sometimes gave the impression he was doing.

Tom Herman:

I think trust was the biggest factor in the evolution of our relationship. I think Cardale understood that we would always have his back as a family. But we would also hold him to extremely high standards. Michelle played a big part in that. Cardale was raised with only a few male role models in his life, namely Ted Ginn. And I think that Michelle constantly calling him, checking on him, providing love and support, etc., really proved to Cardale just how much we cared about him. Some of those phone conversations regarding academics were heated at times, but we really cared about him being successful all-around.

One story that stands out to my wife took place the summer before the 2014 season. We had a quarterback barbecue at our house. A neighbor boy came over to play and asked Braxton and J. T. for an autograph, leaving out Cardale. Although Cardale did not act upset or offended, it hurt my wife's feelings. She told the boy to go back and ask for Cardale's autograph as well. Michelle told him, "You're going to want his autograph someday."

Some of it was just because I refused to "play the game" when it came to my work with academic tutors. My grades were solid. I even earned Scholar-Athlete status that year for having a GPA of 3.0 or better. But we got a weekly score based on our tutoring sessions. I think our standard for an acceptable score was a 7 or 8. I kept getting 4s and 5s because of my inattentiveness. Coach Meyer chastised me, telling me no other quarterback was getting such low scores. His comment pissed me off so much. Until then, I had prepared in case I had to play in a game. We had worksheets we had to fill out late in the week that showed we knew what to do against our opponent in different situations. I'd taken those seriously. But now I was in a deep funk. *Screw this shit*, I figured. I was so over it. I was not going to buy into their thinking that everybody had to do everything one way—the same way—to be successful. I was like, *Whatever. It ain't happening for me anyway, so why am I here wasting my time? This is how they value me right now, so screw football.*

Did they think I was going to go through long days of classes and practice and homework and go sit with a tutor and act like I wanted to be there? I was already handling my academics, and they thought I was supposed to be happy about them being my babysitter? My attitude about the tutoring might not have been the greatest, but did I get my work done? Yes. Well, they needed to shut the fuck up, then. I didn't care if my tutor was unhappy with me that day or if I dozed off during a session. I didn't care if they thought I didn't want to be there. The truth was, I didn't want to be there, and I wasn't going to lie about it. Football players have long days with classes, practice, and meetings. I might have gotten an A on a homework assignment but was criticized because I didn't bring it to my tutor before submitting it. It didn't make sense to me.

Coach Herman kept telling me that as a quarterback at Ohio State, I had to carry myself a certain way. But I could see that other guys on the team who were playing at a high level didn't have the best grades or tutor reports, and coaches didn't seem to come down as hard on them. I'd get chewed out and put back on Dawn Patrol. Coach Herman became so exasperated with me that he devised creative ways of trying to discipline me. Times have changed. If he tried some of the things now that he did to me then, he probably wouldn't get away with it. In some strange way, I think that strengthened our relationship. Michelle became so concerned that she came down from Cleveland to express her frustrations with Coach Meyer and Coach Herman with how some discipline was handled. That meeting was very uncomfortable, even though I didn't say one word. Coach Herman explained his rationale—that they had tried other ways of punishing me, and he was running out of things to make me understand the standard I was expected to maintain. I never made excuses for my actions. If I was asked why I skipped a class and the reason was that I was tired, I said it. If I was late because I couldn't find parking, I'd say so. I didn't have hard feelings about it. I didn't think, *Oh, Herman's a racist* because he was hard on me. I didn't think that then and still don't.

My attitude might have hit rock bottom before the Purdue game, which was two weeks after my infamous tweet. I'd gotten another bad report from the tutors, and Coach Herman made me stay back after we broke the meeting before one of our practices. He expressed disappointment and told me my playing future at Ohio State was up in the air. He said my inconsistency off the field could lead to inconsistency on it. He didn't question my talent. But he did question my trustworthiness and maturity. In my mind, though, I figured if my time came to play, I'd be ready and shock the world.

The next day, I got another score of 4 from the tutors. I was so discouraged. I didn't feel wanted in the place I had always wanted to call home. That's all I could think about during practice. I knew I wasn't going to get a single rep. I couldn't help but think about Coach Tressel, and I believed that things would be going so much better for me if he were still the coach. *He never would have treated me like this,* I thought. That's what was on my mind that day instead of having my focus on practice. Coach Meyer must have sensed that I wasn't paying attention. After one play, he came up from behind me and asked me what play we had just run. I had no clue. All I could do was stammer, "Um, um, um," as I looked at him with a blank expression. He walked away in disbelief. "Hey, Tom, your quarterback didn't know what play you guys just ran," he yelled from the sideline so everyone could hear. It was so embarrassing.

Not only had I let myself down, but I had also made Coach Herman look bad. Honestly, though, I was kind of happy he got yelled at after all the yelling he'd done at me.

I couldn't wait for practice to end, but when it did, Coach Meyer came storming into the locker room, a place he seldom came. Guys knew it had to be something bad. He told me to come to his office after I showered. *Did I just have my last practice here?* I wondered. I took a long shower and then walked to Coach Meyer's office. "Sit down," he said. The meeting didn't last long, but he read me the riot act. "What would I tell the team if I had to put you in a game?" he asked. "How could you expect me to put you in the huddle and lead grown men?" I'd heard this before from Coach Herman, but it was a little different coming from the head duck. Coach Meyer wanted me to understand that I could be only one or two plays from having to go into a game.

But I was so buried on the depth chart that I thought that would never happen. About the only reps I got were on the scout team, running the opponent's plays. I was "live," meaning defensive players could hit me. And I got hammered. Some of the offensive linemen trying to protect me were walk-ons, guys who were never going to play meaningful snaps in a game. One time we were short on offensive linemen and we went with only four of them. The guys on defense didn't kill me, but there were a few times when John Simon, who was our best defensive player, or Garrett Goebel pushed me over.

As the Purdue game approached, I became completely discouraged. It was the first time I didn't prepare as if I were going to play. Zero preparation, other than going through the motions in practice and in the meeting room. I didn't even fill out the pregame worksheet. I lied and said I'd left it in my hotel room when I was supposed to turn it in.

We were big favorites against Purdue, but the Boilermakers led most of the game. Then Braxton got hurt late in the third quarter when he was tackled hard on the sideline after a long run. An ambulance took him to the hospital. With Kenny Guiton in the game, I was now next in line. Coach Meyer's words about being a play away had become a reality. Then at one point, Kenny had some sort of malfunction with his helmet. It looked like he'd have to leave the game to get it fixed. My heart started racing in panic. *Oh, my God. I don't even know what style of defense Purdue is playing. I don't know anything*, I thought. I'm pretty sure that if I'd had to play, all I would have been trusted to do was hand the ball off to running back Carlos Hyde. But I think I would have been so nervous I probably would have fumbled the snap.

When Kenny had the helmet issue and it looked like I might have to go into the game, Coach Meyer looked at me with a withering stare. It felt like he was staring through my soul. I put my helmet on and tried to be super attentive, but I was nervous as hell. My teeth might as well have been chattering. Fortunately, Kenny's helmet problem got fixed, and he didn't miss a play. Trailing 22–14, he led us to a last-minute touchdown on a pass to wide receiver Chris Fields and then a two-point-conversion pass to tight end Jeff Heuerman to take it to overtime. We won it 29–22 in OT. It was the closest call for us that undefeated season, and it was a turning point for me. I was scared straight. I never wanted to feel the way I did when I thought I was going to have to play and was completely unprepared.

In the locker room, I was thankful I didn't have to play and grateful Kenny had risen to the occasion. But I couldn't help thinking, *What if Kenny'd had the same mindset I'd had? What if he didn't take his mental reps seriously this week?* He always carried himself like a starting quarterback. He was as involved in meetings and game-planning as Braxton was. If he hadn't been, there's no way he would have been able to come up clutch when the team needed him most. As I sat in the locker room, something clicked in my head. I vowed to develop a routine. I vowed that I would carry myself as a starter so that if I ever got my chance, I'd be ready.

We finished the season with a victory over Michigan in the Horseshoe. Because we'd been banned from postseason play because of the tattoo scandal, this was our last game, so there was extra emotion for this one, especially after losing to Michigan in 2011. After we won, the fans stormed onto the field and went crazy, surrounding all the players. I couldn't take a step without someone wanting a picture, even though I hadn't even played. I've always been someone to take pictures or interact with fans. I never turn down that stuff. I'm sure there were other players who were also swamped by the throng of fans crowding the field. By the time I got to the locker room, Coach Meyer had already given his postgame speech and most of the players were already gone. I saw a few people criticizing me for that on social media. "Who does this kid think he is? He doesn't want to go in and celebrate with his team." Even after a victory over hated Michigan, it seemed like I couldn't win.

Chapter 9

CONTINUING TO GROW

As you could guess, my end-of-the-season evaluations after 2012 were not pretty. Coaches told me I had the talent but had to figure it out between the ears. They wanted me to show growth every day. I looked at it as a fresh start. For all the bumps in the road, I had survived a year in the system and now understood it. My confidence began growing late in the 2012 season during Sunday night practices when backups got the reps while the starters from the previous day's game rested. I'd done well enough in those to know I could play at this level, and my evaluation showed the coaches thought so too.

Going into 2013, Braxton was clearly the starter, with Kenny Guiton as his backup. Kenny was a senior. If Braxton had a great season, he probably would enter the NFL Draft. That meant I could see a realistic path to being the starter in 2014. My whole thing was to train, get my body right, bust my ass, and separate myself from whomever they brought in. I also knew that in our spread offense, quarterbacks were put at risk because we were often asked to run the ball. Braxton had been banged up quite a bit in 2012. There was a real chance I could play in 2013. After the Purdue scare, I vowed to be prepared if that happened.

In the year since I enrolled, my body had transformed. Again, we didn't really have a weight-training program at Glenville, certainly not like high school programs do now. I weighed only 180 or 190 pounds when I got to Columbus as a freshman. With Ohio State's training table and strength program, and just naturally filling out, I gained about 60 pounds—mostly muscle—and now weighed between 240 and 250 pounds.

I was comfortable with my frame, but it made it tougher when winter workouts started. Conditioning started early because we didn't have a bowl game. Coach Meyer had gone to the BCS National Championship Game between Alabama and Notre Dame. We would have been in that game if we'd been eligible. We would have played Notre Dame, the only other undefeated team in 2012. I know we would have beaten the Fighting Irish, though we wouldn't have been good enough to beat Alabama, which crushed them. Watching Alabama's domination showed Coach Meyer the gap between us and Alabama, and he had Coach Mick ramp up our off-season conditioning program. We'd be chasing Alabama, and "The Chase" became our catch phrase that 2013 season.

In our workouts, players within a position group competed against each other. One thing I hated about our coaching staff was the way they played mental games with the players. It was like if you didn't win every single drill, you sucked and couldn't play here. Well, no matter what I did or how hard I tried, I was not going to beat Braxton Miller in a three-cone drill. He was beating defensive backs and other really fast guys. I had 60 pounds on everyone in my group. I didn't give a flying fuck what the coaches would say about not winning my drills; I just wanted to keep closing the gap. I could tell my overall endurance was much better than it had been, and I was hitting the times I needed in drills. Still, the coaches kept pushing.

One day we had a conditioning drill where we were put in small teams and had to collectively beat a certain time. All the guys in my group were like, "C'mon, Dale. We need you, baby." We had to do the drill four times, and afterward, I was bent over at the knees trying to catch my breath. Coach Herman started yelling, "You better not start this shit this year, Dale! You said you were going to change!" I wasn't going to take that unchallenged. I knew I was in better shape. "You better get the fuck away from me with that shit!" I answered back. "I ain't gonna hear that shit again." I was like, *Leave me alone.* When I was on the field, I wanted to feel my guys. I had their backs, and they had mine. I was leading the show, and that was the only thing that mattered to me.

I didn't really start playing for a coach (as opposed to playing for my teammates and myself) until later in my career there, because honestly, I just didn't have great relations with them. I didn't give a fuck about them. I knew this was a business. I knew they'd leave if they got a better opportunity. I knew they'd try to recruit guys to take my spot eventually. So I played for my teammates, not my coaches. My teammates could see the growth in me. They knew I'd do anything for them, and they would do the same for me. Having that knowledge, I wasn't going to let coaches mindfuck me anymore, saying I could never play there or that I sucked. I was so far past that. They would just be wasting their breath.

The first Ohio State coach who made a real impact on me wasn't Coach Herman or Coach Meyer. It was tight ends coach Tim Hinton. We were in the parking lot at the Woody early in 2013 when he came up to me and said, "Man, listen. You've got the talent. But stop sitting back and waiting for your turn." He was right about my mentality. I knew I wasn't going to beat out Braxton or Kenny. But Coach Hinton told me to push myself anyway. I'll never forget those words. It made me realize that there was someone at Ohio State who did notice my ability and saw something in me.

As I said, my real competition in 2013 wasn't really Braxton and Kenny. They were clearly ahead of me. I knew I'd be competing with incoming freshman J. T. Barrett from Wichita Falls, Texas. Even though I had been at Ohio State a year and J. T. was coming off an ACL tear and the plan was for him to redshirt, I understood one thing: J. T. had been recruited by the current OSU coaching staff, and I hadn't. J. T. was their handpicked guy. I was just the guy they inherited.

In that sense, I identified quite a bit with Kenny, and Kenny did with me. He'd gotten a scholarship offer very late in the recruiting process only when other quarterbacks they'd targeted fell through. Kenny's only other scholarship offer was from Prairie View A&M. But Kenny proved to be a great find. He didn't have Braxton's legs or arm, but he was a true student of the game. I even think Kenny should have been the starter in 2012, even though we went 12–0 with Braxton. Kenny was mentally so far ahead of the rest of us in the room. As a quarterback, as a leader, as a vocal guy, it was Kenny. I think he had more intangibles to lead our team at that time than Braxton did. Braxton was still a young player, still trying to learn the system and trying to learn college defenses. Kenny was so much more advanced when it came to being an overall quarterback, other than the physical stuff.

Braxton and I had a good relationship, but I had a really close one with Kenny. We both played on the scout team and would cheer each other on. He could see a guy like me with all the ability to play there. Clearly, I didn't get it all done off the field with some of the little things I was still doing. But Kenny went through some of the same issues in his career. He could see that what I feared would happen to me had happened to him: younger, more preferred quarterbacks were being recruited over us. Kenny knew the game at that point. He was a great mentor. I wish the transfer portal had been around for him. He would have had unbelievable opportunities. He'd have proven he was plenty capable.

When I think about the 2013 season, what stands out more than anything I did was what happened with Kenny. In our opener against Buffalo, Kenny threw a touchdown pass after Braxton went out with a leg cramp. The next week against San Diego State, Braxton sprained his knee on our first series. Kenny played well the rest of the game to lead us to a 42–7 win.

Braxton missed the next two games. We traveled to Berkeley to play Cal, and Kenny threw for four touchdowns and 276 yards in our 52–34 win. The next day, we were in the locker room getting ready for practice, and the TV was showing Florida A&M's game from the day before. I honestly thought it was a high school game. The players were so much smaller than us. But someone said that was our next opponent. I was like, "Oh my God, it's going to be a massacre. I hope no one on that team gets hurt."

I also knew that if the game were as lopsided as it should be, I'd finally get to make my Ohio State playing debut. I was right. Kenny tied a school record with six touchdown passes, and then I got my chance. Playing in the Horseshoe for the first time was pretty sweet. The thing about Ohio State fans is that most of them will stick around until the end.

My debut didn't quite go as scripted. On one of my first plays, I ran a quarterback sweep. Wide receiver James Clark was blocking for me. As I got close to him, I don't know if I panicked or what, but I could see I was going to collide with him. I slowed down, closed my eyes, and braced for the hit. I rolled up on James's leg and it broke. I felt so bad for him.

A few plays later, when I clapped to signal for the snap, my hands felt a little weird. Running back Ezekiel "Zeke" Elliott, then a freshman backup, ran for a touchdown. When I got back to the sideline, I noticed my hand was red. I thought, *What the hell is that?* I rinsed it off with water. Coach Herman was on the sideline at this point because the game was such a blowout that they had coaches normally upstairs in the booth stay on the field during the second half. He was talking to me, and I could feel my hand pulsing. I looked again and saw it was blood—my blood. It turned out I'd ripped my right hand open stiff-arming a tackler on my first drive. I asked a trainer for a Band-Aid, and when he saw my hand, he gasped, "Oh my God! You need stitches." I looked down and could see the bone. "Oh, shit! That's my bone?" I said. They put Kenny back in while I went to the locker room and got stitches and a painkiller shot. I put a glove on my hand and went back in and finished the game. I didn't throw a pass but did run eight times, including a 10-yard score for our final touchdown.

I don't know what kind of conversations the coaches had with Kenny after he went back to being a backup the next week when Braxton returned. I can only imagine there wasn't one, or if there was, Kenny wasn't happy with how it went. His demeanor became deflated. Our team kept rolling, though. We won the rest of our games and went to the Big Ten Football Championship Game against Michigan State. If we'd won, we'd have gone to the national title game in the last year of the BCS system before the start of the four-team College Football Playoff in 2014. But we lost 34–24 in Indianapolis in the league championship. We fell behind 17–0, scored the next 24 points, but then allowed Michigan State to score the final 17. I know Kenny was really bothered by the loss against Michigan State. I'm not putting that loss on Braxton at all. But we as an offense did have some boneheaded mistakes in that game.

I think by then Kenny felt extremely disrespected by the staff. I really saw that on display when we started practice in Columbus for the Orange Bowl against Clemson. You could see that he thought he'd wasted his career there. Coaches used to call him Coach Guiton. It was meant as a compliment, but I think Kenny took it as a backhanded one. I think his mindset was: *You're telling me I'm smart. You're telling me I've got the ability. You're telling me I've got all the intangibles. But I can't play. You're trying to pull the wool over my eyes. "Oh, he's super smart." Well, let me continue to show that.*

Before we went down to south Florida, I think KG was just fed up—with the way his career turned out, with the coaching staff, and with some lies he had been told. He was frustrated this was his last game and he probably wasn't going to play in it. Kenny was just going through the motions in practice. I remember him and Coach Herman having words, and Coach Herman saying, "Kenny, don't burn bridges." In practice, it was like Kenny threw the ball to the defense intentionally. In ball-security drills, he'd just let the guy slap it out of his hands. J. T. and I would look at each other like, *What the fuck?*

When we got to Florida, Kenny changed his demeanor and was still there for the team. But I can only imagine he felt betrayed by the staff. Then in the Orange Bowl, Braxton injured his shoulder early. But Kenny still didn't get an opportunity. We lost to Clemson in a back-and-forth game that ended when Braxton threw an interception in the final minute. His shoulder clearly affected him. But we had no idea how Braxton's injury would affect the 2014 season and the role I'd be thrust into.

Chapter 10

READY TO LEAVE, UNTIL . . .

When spring practice for the 2014 season began, my focus was on winning the backup job. I knew that finally I'd get my opportunity. Kenny Guiton had graduated, and Braxton Miller's surgery following his shoulder injury in the Orange Bowl kept him out of spring practice, though we all assumed he'd be ready for preseason camp. My competition was J. T. Barrett, as I'd predicted. When J. T. had enrolled the previous year, I knew he was brought in to be the heir apparent to Braxton. You might think that would have affected our personal relationship. But we became very close friends. That really developed in the latter half of the 2013 season and definitely at the Orange Bowl. We roomed together there and really connected. Going into the 2014 season, our relationship really ramped up. We truly wanted the best for each other. We both dealt with the same thing when it came to coaches always being on our asses. One day, you're the greatest. The next, you suck. We helped each other get through that. We also recognized that when one of us played well, the other one would be spurred to raise the level of his game. Iron sharpens iron.

Our personalities were complete opposites. J. T.'s father, Joe, was in the military, and you could tell that from the way J. T. was raised. I will argue that I was one of the first people to get him out of his shell. J. T. can be, "Yes, sir. No, sir." He walked a straight line. At first, I was like, "Are you a robot or something?"

J. T. Barrett:

The military hard-discipline thing wasn't really where I got it. I think it was more so because my parents grew up in big families. My mom was one of 12. My dad was one of 9. They just got tough love. I think I got it from my mom. My dad wasn't around the whole time because he was in the military. He moved around a lot. We just stayed in Wichita Falls.

Over time, I think he got better at having that on-and-off switch. Me, I'm one way unless you piss me off. I'm never going to be too serious to where it's uncomfortable. I'm going to be serious enough to make sure we do what we've got to do. J. T., when he's in a leadership situation or a team environment, if you're not doing your job damn near to a *T*, you're probably going to be uncomfortable around J. T. because of the way he carries himself. There's nothing wrong with that. He's a perfectionist in his own way, a hardworking guy who demands excellence from everybody around him.

J. T. Barrett:

Honestly, our relationship was like a big brother situation. I came in as the younger guy—young and dumb—and Cardale would look out for me. I was fortunate to have a father. He would give me little nuggets of advice. He told me I could learn something from everybody so I didn't have to learn everything by going through it myself. Cardale had been at Ohio State for a year, so once I got comfortable, I'd ask Cardale things, and he'd guide me, whether it was about football, school, tutoring, whatever. Cardale always looked out for me. I can't say there's one time we had a bad vibe with each other or ever had a time when we were mad at each other. It was just a real good bond from the get-go. It's always been like a brother relationship.

I began spring ball taking the first reps with the starters. Coach Meyer called me a changed guy and said I'd earned that slot. From everything I know, nothing changed through the spring. Our 15 practices ended with the spring game, which is always a big deal at Ohio State and usually draws a big crowd. One of the things that got the fans juiced up was a pregame circle drill. That's something Coach Meyer started. Two guys would line up, surrounded by teammates, and try to take the other down in a quick burst. Because of my size, I'd been matched up against linebackers and tight ends when we'd done the circle drill and other things like it in the spring. But now Coach Meyer wanted me to go against J. T. Poor J. T.; he didn't have a chance. I outweighed him by about 30 pounds. I don't think he'd even done a single circle drill that spring. I think the first two reps, we took it easy on each other. A good little pop, and that was it. Coach Meyer was on to us. "Don't let off!" he yelled. "Don't let off!" Oh, he caught us. So I did what I had to do and buried J. T. He was like, "Why'd you do me like that?" We laughed it off. As for the spring game itself, J. T. had the better performance, but those scrimmages were primarily for the developmental guys. It was unusual for prominent players like Joey Bosa and Ezekiel Elliott to play much in a spring game.

Besides, based on my performance and my understanding of where we stood, I had a better overall spring than J. T. *OK, cool*, I thought. *I'm going to be the backup to Braxton for the season*. The coaches didn't tell me that directly, but from our grading sheets and everything we'd done, I was putting two and two together.

J. T. Barrett:

Cardale had a really good spring. He grew a lot, week by week, each practice. Me, on the other hand, I was just trying to figure it out. I was all over the place. My eyes were all over the place. I was nervous. I struggled for sure. Coming out of that spring, there was no doubt that Cardale was the backup and I was third-string.

I didn't think J. T. and I would continue our battle in training camp. But Coach Meyer decided to open the competition again. I never had a conversation with him. I wish he'd communicated more with me about it so at least I would have known. I got discouraged and somewhat in my own head. It didn't help that often my offensive linemen were overmatched. A backup trying to block Joey Bosa? I was trying to make the most of every rep when I knew the deck was stacked against me. I think it just boiled down to the fact that I just wasn't *their* guy. They had recruited J. T. They had *inherited* me. About two weeks before the season, Coach Meyer told the media that J. T. had moved ahead of me.

Urban Meyer:

If I remember right, Cardale was the No. 2 in the spring. But in training camp, it changed. It was obvious that J. T. was not as talented as Cardale, but one of my beliefs at that position is that leadership is more important than talent. J. T. was such a natural leader and J. T. gave us a little bit more of a dual threat. And just his attention to detail helped push him ahead of Cardale. But it was very close.

Coach Meyer didn't tell me directly that I was third-string behind J. T. Maybe he thought I should have inferred that by our reps. By then J. T. was getting more of them, but I was still getting some with the starters. But nobody told me who was going to be the backup. If I had known I wasn't going to be, I probably would have left that fall. With J. T. the clear backup and a year behind me in eligibility, I would have had no path to play unless I transferred.

Tyvis Powell:

He was pissed. Pissed. Cardale was very upset. He was running with the threes, and he was a guy who was in year 3. His demeanor just changed. It seemed like he had given up a little bit, to be honest with you. That's how I took it.

A day or two later, Braxton dropped back to pass in practice. The quarterbacks stood right behind the play, so I had a good view. I think we were running an RPO (run-pass option) out pattern. As Braxton threw, he went down, holding his arm like it was numb. I thought at first somebody had hit him. It looked like he had a stinger, the way he was holding his arm. But he had torn his labrum. He was grunting and screaming. Braxton was a tough guy. He wasn't one of those players who'd milk an injury for sympathy. I knew this was serious.

Obviously, my first thoughts were for Braxton. I just felt extremely bad for him. He hadn't been around much of spring practice because he was doing rehab. I knew how much work he had put in to get to that point. I knew how hard they were pushing him to get healthy. Braxton was a Heisman Trophy favorite, and obviously a huge part of our team. Now, he clearly was gone. The injury just sucked the air out of the whole team the rest of practice.

Tyvis Powell:

Man, that was a sad day. You've watched a Heisman candidate, who's electric, who could do things in practice that made you say "Good Lord," who I had watched dominate for two seasons. And he was gone. I made the mistake of going online and seeing the Vegas odds. I think we'd been the second or third favorite to win the national championship, and we dropped all the way to like 20. I was thinking that our season might be over before it started. I think that was the general response on the team.

The next day, we were still in shock. Coach Meyer gave a speech saying that we had to hit the ground running, we couldn't let this hiccup derail our season before it even started. This was 11 or 12 days before our season opener against Navy in Baltimore. We had already spent a lot of time in the summer trying to prepare for Navy's tricky triple-option offense. Now we had to break in a new starting quarterback. I realized it wasn't going to be me. J. T. pretty much got all the first-team reps in practice.

J. T. Barrett:

That camp, I was playing a lot better, and Cardale was struggling. There were times where I had the twos and we were going against the ones and we were just driving the ball. I'd told myself after the spring to kind of have an "Eff it" mindset and not overthink things and just go out and play. Each practice, it was just a little bit better for me. My ball placement was at a high level back then. That camp in particular, I was placing the ball where I wanted it.

It was discouraging. I started to understand why Kenny Guiton's demeanor at the end was the way it was: Lack of communication. A feeling of disrespect. Knowing that you're good enough but not having the opportunity to show it. I was in such a unique situation because clearly neither one of us was proven at that point. J. T. had not played at all in 2013, and I'd only played in mop-up time. I remember saying something to Coach Herman like, "Dude, what's the deal? I thought I had a good spring. I thought I had a good camp." He just told me I was playing well and to stay ready.

Tom Herman:

With that little time before the first game, we felt like whoever was going to be the starter needed to get the maximum number of reps leading up to the game. And because J. T. was slightly ahead of Cardale, he was the logical choice to start in the opener.

Urban Meyer:

Tom and I had nonstop conversation about it, but we just felt J. T. was the No. 2 guy. It was his spot, and he held on to it. The way J. T. was, the way he worked, he was not going to let go of something like that. With the seriousness he had, he earned respect amongst his teammates real quick.

In the opener against Navy, we struggled. J. T. threw an interception at the end of a long drive in the second quarter and missed a few completable balls. We managed only two field goals in the first half and trailed 7–6 going into halftime. In my mind, I knew I was going to get my shot to do something. I was like, *I'm ready for this shit.* But my name never got called. We, including J. T., played better in the second half. Linebacker Darron Lee recovered a fumble and returned it for a touchdown, and we pulled away to win 34–17. Of course, I was happy for J. T. and for the success of the team. Coach Herman congratulated J. T. I was sitting right next to him in the locker room, and Coach Herman didn't say one word to me. Nothing. I was like, *Whatever.*

The next week was our home opener against Virginia Tech. The Horseshoe had added additional seating with a stadium expansion in the off-season, so this was the largest crowd in OSU history. Ohio State hadn't lost at home to an unranked team in 32 years, but the prime-time game was a disaster. Virginia Tech defensive coordinator Bud Foster used a Bear defense that clogged the running game and dared us to throw. We couldn't. The coaches admitted afterward that they were unprepared for what Foster threw at us.

J. T. Barrett:

We didn't have a plan for what they were doing.

Receivers couldn't get separation and dropped passes. J. T. missed on a couple deep balls and was sacked seven times. I'd have bet my life savings going into the fourth quarter that I was going to get put in. I was thinking, *Here's my chance.* But again, nothing. *You've got to be fucking shitting me,* I thought. J. T. completed only 9 of 29 passes for

219 yards and threw three interceptions, including a pick-six late in the fourth quarter that sealed Virginia Tech's 35–21 win. No personal knock on J. T.'s performance, but the competitor in me couldn't help but feel we would have had a different outcome if I'd gotten in the game.

J. T. Barrett:

After Virginia Tech, we started splitting reps again, and we didn't stop splitting reps until, I want to say, after Cincinnati two weeks later. The week after Virginia Tech, we played Kent State. We won 66–0, but I remember there was a play, a third-and-short when Devin Smith beat his man on a go route. But Kent State blitzed through the A gap and I threw the ball away as I got hit. All Coach Meyer saw was Devin win his route and thought it should have been a touchdown. When I got to the sideline, he just said to me, "Man, you're not that good." I just looked at the man, and then he walked away. And that was it.

But I enjoyed playing for Coach Meyer. He was very straightforward. The more you helped the team, the better you were treated. And if you weren't helping us, you were hurting us. It was real clear. He expected people to work really hard, and it didn't matter who you were. He expected a lot from everybody. And I think that's why when we lost, it would hurt so bad. I never saw a person take losing like Coach Meyer. Like, I think he would get physically ill.

J. T. threw six touchdown passes against Kent State. I didn't get in until mop-up time. After splitting reps in practice all week and then barely playing, it was discouraging.

> *Tyvis Powell:*
>
> *That was a very depressing thing. I'm sure he would tell you that if the roles were flipped and Cardale was the starter [against Virginia Tech], they'd have put J. T. in for sure. But when he didn't get a chance when J. T. was struggling, the writing was pretty much on the wall. They didn't trust him to go into games like that. That would hurt anybody. "Y'all see he's struggling, and you're still not going to give me a chance to go in the game and prove something and see if I can make something happen?" That lets you know they're riding with him the rest of the year. It was his third year and he hadn't really touched the field. What was he supposed to do? When Cardale went into a depression, you kinda saw a "don't-give-an-eff" attitude. That was Cardale's version of depression.*

At that point, I was ready to fill out the paperwork to transfer out of Ohio State. But Coach Herman told me he wouldn't sign my release papers. He explained that you don't want to have a quarterback battle during the season because you want your quarterback to feel you're going to win or lose with him. You don't want your starter to look over his shoulder. That really resonated with me, because I thought that if I was ever in that position, I'd want my team and coaches to think the same way. (No way could I have known that a year later I'd be in that same situation.)

The next week, we played at Penn State in front of their famous White Out crowd. For those who've never had a chance to experience a White Out at Penn State, it's one of the most energetic, electrifying atmospheres in all of sports. A crowd of 100,000-plus all waving white pom-poms, screaming almost nonstop and cheering on the Nittany Lions. By far one of the loudest stadiums I've been in. If the hostile environment wasn't enough, Penn State was one of the best teams in the Big Ten year in and year out.

We jumped to a 17–0 lead, but on the last play of the first half, J. T. sprained his knee. At halftime, I was sitting next to him in the locker room, and his knee was not good at all. Coach Meyer came up to him and said, "Can you go?" He said he could. On the first possession of the third quarter, J. T. threw a pick-six. Penn State came back to tie the game. There was a third-down play when J. T. got sacked and you could tell he had trouble moving. On the next possession, we had a third-and-1. They put me in for a quarterback power dive. Penn State was expecting it, and I got stuffed for no gain. That was my only snap. The game went to overtime. Penn State scored first, but J. T. gutted out a couple of nice runs for the tying touchdown. In double overtime, J. T. bulled his way into the end zone after getting hit by two linemen to put us back ahead. Joey Bosa clinched the win with a fourth-down sack. That was probably the game that really solidified J. T.'s status as our leader. We knew he was injured and still led us to a hard-fought victory. If there was any doubt before, it was gone now. This was J. T.'s team.

Because he was only a redshirt freshman and it was just the start of his career, there was no place for me. I accepted this. I was still going to prepare to be ready if needed. But in my mind, I decided that the 2014 season would be my last as a Buckeye. I wasn't content to spend the rest of my college career as a backup.

J. T. Barrett:

He never really showed around me that he was upset. Those things, I think he kept to himself. He was always very supportive and showed love toward me. He was very helpful. He'd give tips on the sideline just from things he could see from his perspective.

Tom Herman:

Cardale is one of the best teammates I've ever been around, and that's hard to do when you play a position where only one guy plays. I thought he handled it with the utmost maturity and professionalism. He was J. T.'s biggest cheerleader because of the relationship that they had developed. He was also disappointed that he wouldn't be starting and got even more serious about his preparation.

The next week against Illinois, I got to play the entire second half after we led 31–0 at halftime. I threw for the first two touchdowns of my Ohio State career. The first came on a deep ball to Dontre Wilson. That felt good because I had to do some things to set up the defense, and I did them, so that gave me some confidence.

But what I remember most are a couple of encounters with my old high school teammate V'Angelo Bentley. The first came when we used a wildcat formation and I lined up wide. The problem was, I went to the wrong side. We ran a reverse and the runner came my way, so I had to be the lead blocker. Poor V'Angelo, who was at least 50 pounds lighter than I was, was in my way. I just buried him. I took his ass out of bounds, and we scored. The other came on a pass play. As I started to throw, I saw somebody jump in front of me, and the ball came loose, like a spike. I thought it was an incompletion but didn't hear a whistle. V'Angelo picked the ball up and started to run the other way near the Illini sideline. Quarterbacks are told if they're in the open field after a turnover to try to make the guy cut back. That way, a teammate will have a better angle to make the tackle. That's what I tried to do. Then I saw our guard, Billy Price, get absolutely hammered on a crackback block. I saw that and thought, *Fuck. That. Shit. I'm out of here.* I wanted no part of getting drilled like that. So I kind of changed directions and headed toward our sideline. But V'Angelo cut back too. As I looked up, he was right there in front of me. I just drilled him. The funniest thing about it is that the play was ruled an incompletion after review, so all of it was for nothing.

The next week, we had a showdown against Michigan State in East Lansing. I wouldn't play in that game, but it still was one of the most important weeks of my life.

Chapter 11

BECOMING A FATHER

SOMETHING ELSE WAS ON MY MIND that fall, and it transcended football. I was going to become a father. I had started dating Jeaney Durand in the fall semester of our freshman year. She was from Cleveland and was the youngest of four daughters in a loving, smart family. She earned scholarship money for Ohio State by working as a researcher at Case Western Reserve in high school.

We first connected on Facebook the winter I got to Ohio State. We had mutual friends. Jeaney was still at home at the time, so I told her to let me know when she got to campus. When she arrived for orientation, we started hanging out and then went on little dates before we started officially dating. Jeaney was someone I felt I could always talk to about a lot of different things. I think what sparked that was a time I lied to her early in our relationship. Michelle was waiting to move into a new home and was staying with her cousin, who had a really nice house. I lied and told Jeaney that it was our house. I guess I was trying to impress her. But Michelle mentioned in passing that it was just where we were staying temporarily. Jeaney challenged me, asking if I felt I had to lie to her, and told me I didn't.

She told me she'd have my back no matter what. That made me feel comfortable with her, and I began to let my guard down.

We dated for about two and a half years. Then we grew apart for whatever reason—just being young. We decided to take a step back, but we still hung out occasionally while trying to work through some of our relationship issues. Then we found out she was pregnant.

I had a lot of mixed emotions. We weren't together at the time. I always wanted to be married first and then have a family. I also never wanted to have kids by more than one woman, and I was putting that in jeopardy because I wasn't with her anymore. Even though we were still working on our relationship, some of the red flags I saw in it weren't things I thought we could work through. About four months into the pregnancy, we thought maybe it would be better to cut all ties and get an abortion. We even went so far as to go to the first appointment. But we decided not to go forward with the abortion.

The week after the Illinois game, Ohio State played Michigan State in what would be our biggest game of the year. We remembered how the Spartans had ruined our season in the Big Ten championship the year before, and they were favored at home in a prime-time showdown. At this point, we were hitting our groove as a team. I was 100 percent convinced that J. T. was going to win the Heisman. I was kind of on autopilot at that point. I prepared like I would play but accepted that I probably wouldn't. As quarterbacks, we had to get our ankles taped before every practice as a precaution. It was a huge rule at Ohio State. But at our Thursday practice, which was a lighter one than on Tuesdays or Wednesdays, I didn't bother doing that because I wasn't expecting to get any reps other than two plays in the walk-through. Sure enough, during a rep with the backups, we practiced a jump pass. As I came down, I landed on the foot of center Joel Hale and rolled my left ankle. It was badly sprained—the worst injury I've ever had in sports to this day. I didn't fall but was

Running with the opportunity of a lifetime.

Celebrating with Coach Meyer on the sideline during the Wisconsin game.

Big Ten champs at last!

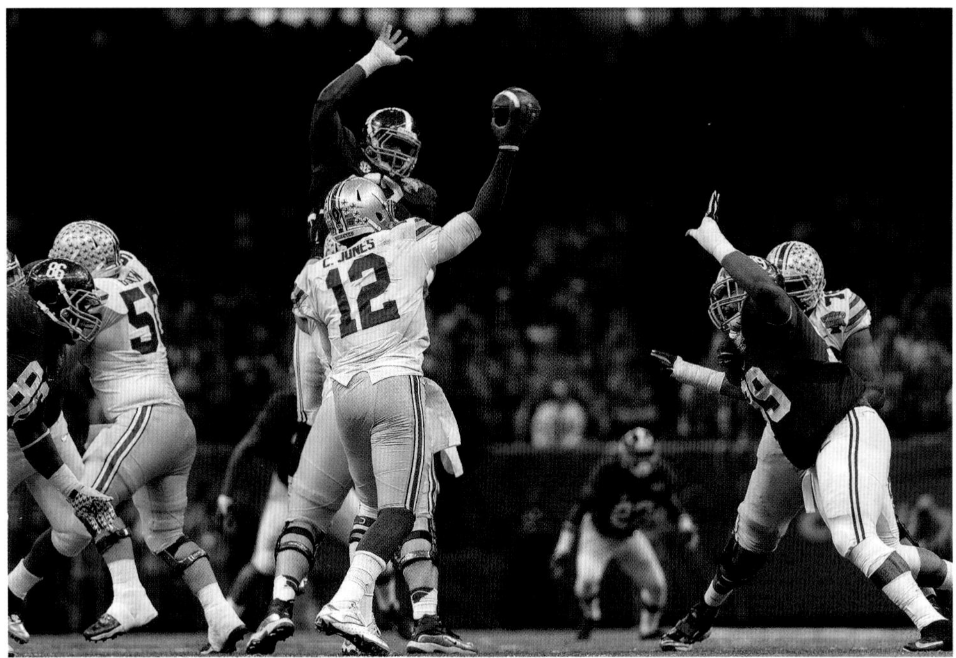

Letting it fly against Alabama in the Sugar Bowl.

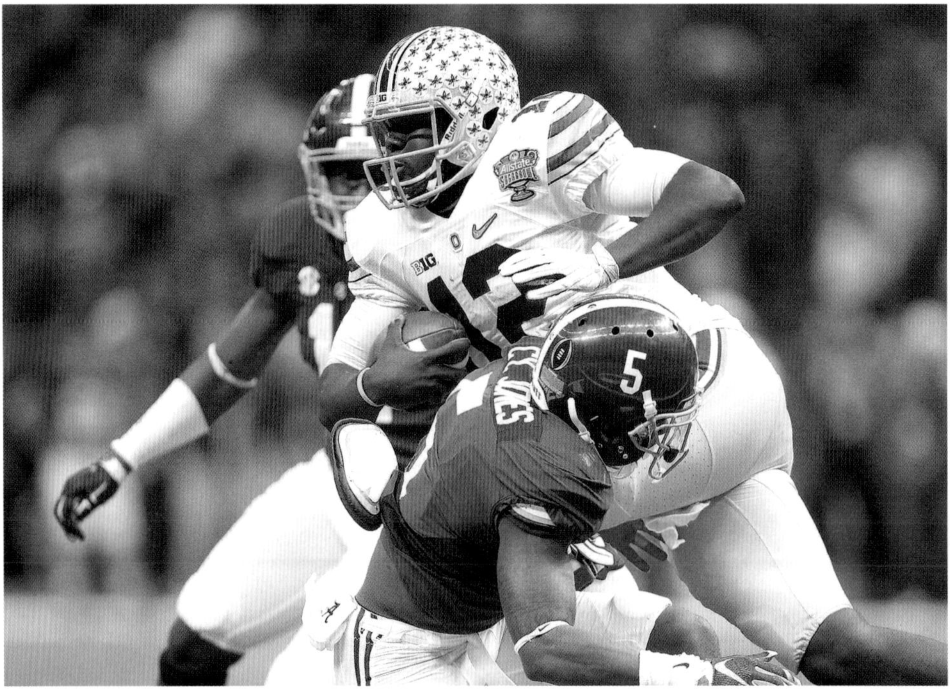

Sometimes you've just gotta use your legs.

Scoring against Oregon in the national championship game.

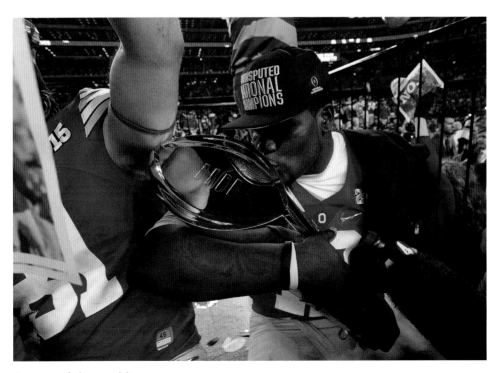

On top of the world!

I began the 2015 season as the starter, but it didn't go as I'd hoped.

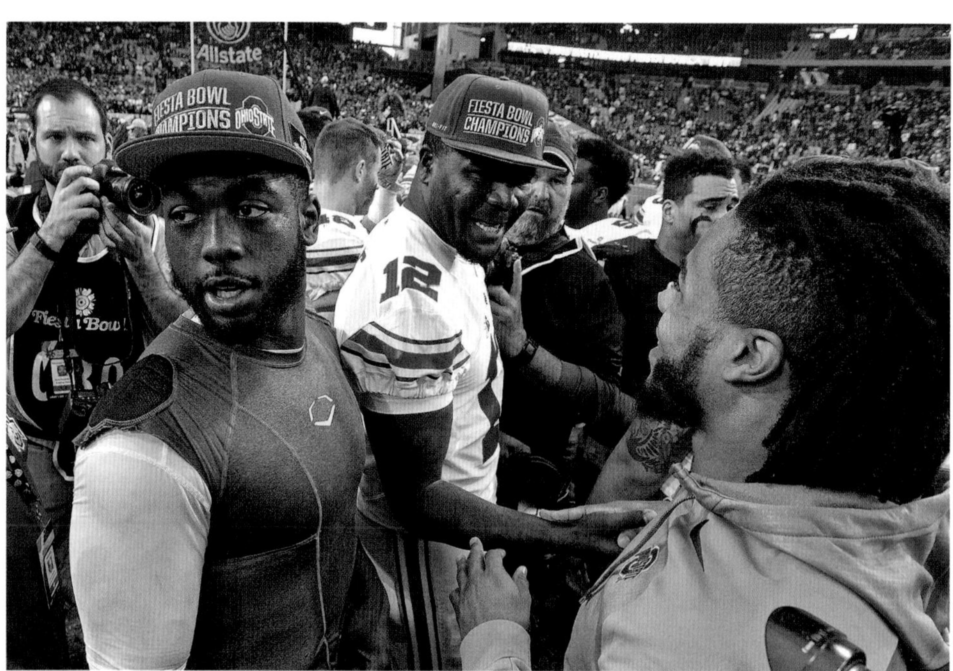

With J. T. Barrett, ending my career as Fiesta Bowl champions.

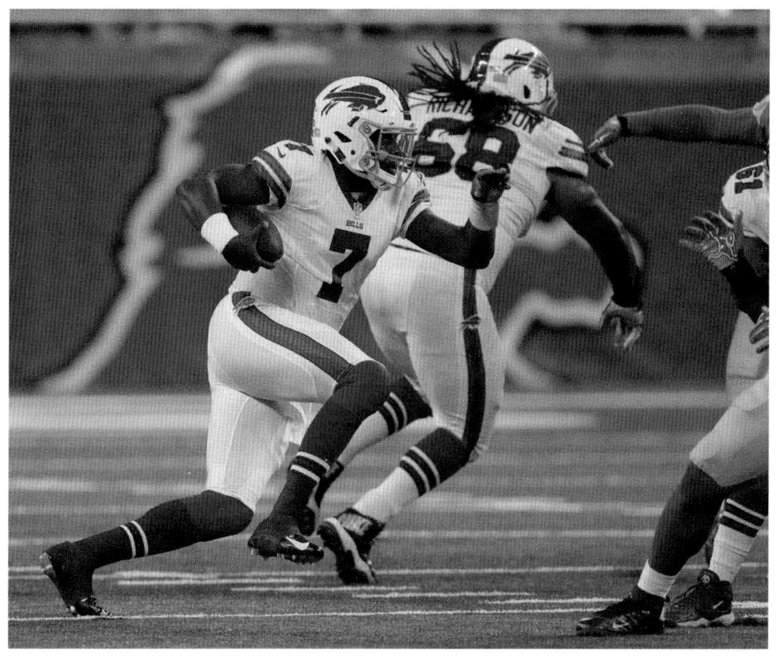

I started my NFL career with the Buffalo Bills in 2016.

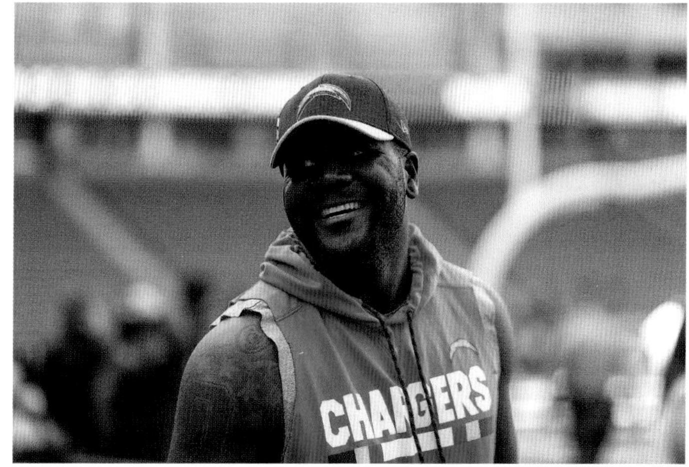

I was traded to the Los Angeles Chargers in my second year.

Going through pre-snap reads in a 2019 preseason game.

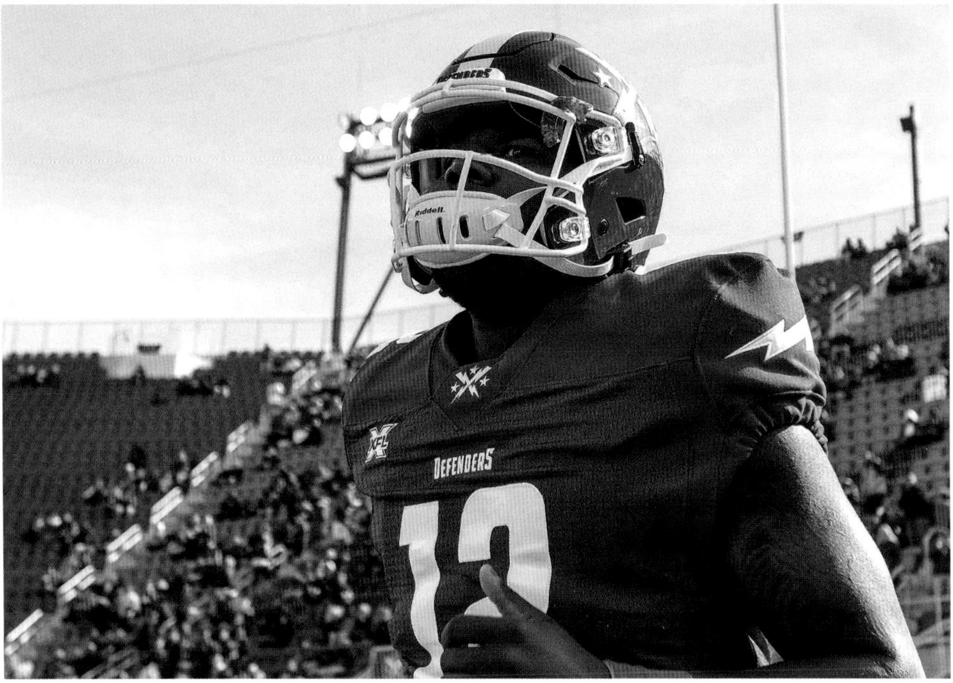

I found a new home in the XFL with the DC Defenders.

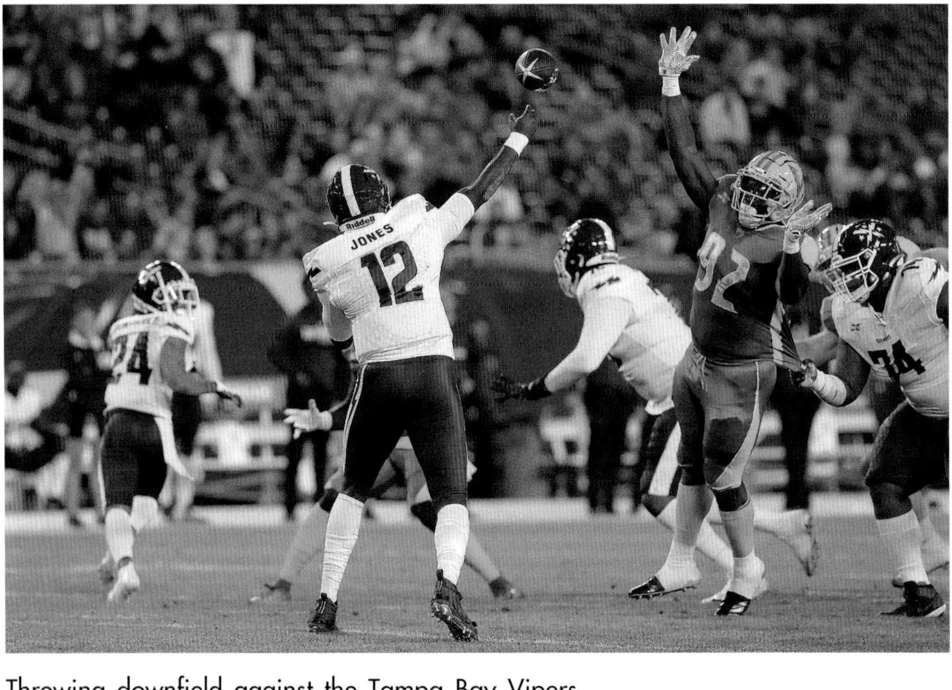

Throwing downfield against the Tampa Bay Vipers.

Advocating for name, image, and likeness rights for student-athletes.

Posing here with Bill's dog Ellie, our unofficial coauthor.

My mom Michelle and me on my college graduation day.

Mom and my youngest son, Owen, Christmas 2019.

Me and my siblings Sheena, Naomi, and Javon, celebrating my first XFL career game and win.

limping. Tom Herman yelled at me, "Tell me you got your ankles taped!" I ignored him as I looked to the sideline to get the next play call. When I did, I looked over and said a quick, "Nope." I was trying to limp to get the snap. He blew the whistle, and he ripped me: "Get the fuck out!" Now the pain was setting in. I was limping to a trainer to get my ankle taped. I said to him, "This thing hurts. I don't think tape is going to do it." We tried to take my shoe and sock off, and the swelling was so bad I couldn't see my foot. I was thinking my ankle must be broken. I got it taped back up. The worst part was having to stand through the rest of practice. I got treatment after practice and got up super early that Friday to get more treatment at 6:00 AM. I had an 8:00 AM class before the team got on the plane at 2:00 PM to go to East Lansing.

Jeaney was back in Cleveland for a checkup. The baby wasn't due for a month. I'd talked to her right after practice Thursday, and everything was great. But when I woke up on Friday, I checked my phone and there were like 42 missed calls. I freaked out. I was thinking something tragic had happened. I had calls from Jeaney, Michelle, my sister, Jeaney's aunt, everyone. Then I got another call from my aunt DeShanae. I answered it. She told me Jeaney had gone into labor. I was like, "What? This is amazing." I went to the Woody just to check in and say that I had to get to Cleveland because my daughter was about to be born. I was in an air cast and on crutches at the time. My ankle was jacked up. They looked at me for a second and then told me to hurry up to Cleveland and get back before the plane left.

I got in my car—a 2006 Dodge Charger. My "'Dalemobile" had 242,000 miles on it, but I loved it. I penny-pinched about $3,000 to buy that thing. It was one of those cars with a really loud engine, but it didn't actually have the power to go anywhere really fast. It did that day. I freaking floored it all the way to Hillcrest Hospital in Mayfield. Normally it's about a two-hour drive between Cleveland and Columbus. I did it in about 90 minutes. I probably got close to

120 miles per hour at times. It was so early that the highway was clear. As I got close to the hospital, I called to find out what room Jeaney was in but couldn't get through to the hospital. When I got there, I asked the receptionist, who told me. I started running to the room, or at least moving as fast as I could on crutches. At a certain point, I just threw the crutches down and limped as fast as I could. I was in so much pain. I finally found the room right when Jeaney was about to start pushing. I made it just in time. My daughter, Chloe, was born at 8:00 AM. After the adrenaline wore off after seeing the baby, the pain set in again. My crutches were somewhere in a hallway, and my foot was *throbbing*. I stayed long enough to make sure everything was good with Jeaney and the baby and hurried back to Columbus. I got a little more treatment and then got on the plane.

As crazy as that time was, I still found time to tweet. I posted something about how it sucks rolling your ankle or having to ice it. Coach Herman was not happy. Why would I give any information like that to an opponent? Just another of the delete-your-tweet orders from him during my career. One of my favorites was when our bus arrived at Michigan Stadium in Ann Arbor in 2013 and I tweeted, "Oh, just pulled up to the shithole." The coaches had banned me from Twitter after the infamous tweet, but they had let me back on because they thought I'd matured. Joke was on them, I guess.

Anyway, back to Michigan State. I wore four layers of protection on my ankle when I dressed for the game. Trainers taped my ankle, put an ankle brace on top of that, and put tape over that. I put my socks on, and they taped over that. I normally wore size 13 cleats, but with so much taping and the brace, I think I had to wear a size 16 or 17 on my left foot. My ankle was so stiff that I actually fell down twice during warm-ups. It felt a little like the Purdue game my freshman year when Kenny Guiton's helmet issue almost forced me to play after I hadn't done my preparation. I was prepared mentally for Michigan State, but who knows what would have happened with my ankle if I'd had to play. Fortunately, I didn't. J. T. and the whole team played great. We overcame some early mistakes and beat Michigan State 49–37. It was really our coming-out party. This was the first year of the College Football Playoff after the Virginia Tech loss. This game was billed as an elimination game. For the first time, a path to the CFP seemed possible, even if it still looked unlikely.

We got back to Columbus about 2:00 AM, and I drove right back to Cleveland to see Jeaney and Chloe. But we had our Sunday afternoon practice back at the Woody, so I drove down for that and went right back to Cleveland. Of course, I had an 8:00 AM class on Monday. Back to Columbus. Thank God my only other Monday class got canceled. Back to Cleveland. I stayed there until I had to drive back for a 10:00 AM class on Tuesday.

That week was such a blur. But when Chloe was born, all I kept thinking was that I wouldn't have missed it for the world. I knew it was going to change my mindset: *Everything I do is for this little thing right here*. I think it put so many things in perspective for me—the way I grew up, all the times I remember that I was hungry or didn't have what I wanted. All that came rushing back at once. I knew I had to do everything I could to make sure she didn't grow up the way I did.

Chapter 12

THE TEAM UP NORTH, AND EVERYTHING CHANGES

CHLOE'S BIRTH CHANGED MY MINDSET and gave me even more of a purpose than I had. But my football situation at Ohio State remained the same. Not that there was any doubt that J. T. was the unquestioned starter before the Michigan State game, but his performance in East Lansing cemented it. He threw for 300 yards and three touchdowns and ran for 86 yards and two more scores.

My ankle healed pretty quickly. Within a couple weeks, I could walk normally and really only felt pain if I cut sharply. But I didn't play in our next two games—a 31–24 win in 15-degree weather and light snow at Minnesota and a 42–27 win at home against Indiana.

Up next: Michigan. To those not in the OSU program, it's hard to describe what our rivalry game means. I personally think there's nothing else in sports like it. In the NFL, you have rivalries in your conference and your division. When I was with the Chargers, the rivalry with the Raiders was pretty intense. I've been to the Iron Bowl with Alabama and Auburn. I've been to a Yankees–Red Sox game. I still say there's nothing like our rivalry. It's crazy how as a player, you almost get lost in it that week. No matter what happened the previous week, nothing else matters. My freshman year, I remember it was like a switch flipped immediately after our 11th game. The following day, our marching band—The Best Damn Band in the Land—came to our practice. Our theme song of the week, LL Cool J's "It's Time for War," played nonstop. Highlights from past games were playing on the screens. Michigan's maize-and-blue jerseys were put on the floor for us to walk on.

When I was really little, I actually preferred Michigan. Blue is my favorite color, and Michigan then had the upper hand in the rivalry in the 1990s before Coach Tressel was hired. But then I understood, with the help of relatives who were Buckeyes fans, the error of my ways, and my allegiance switched. I became an Ohio State fan because of the Ohio State–Michigan game. I didn't care about watching Ohio State vs. Illinois or Ohio State vs. Indiana or even Ohio State vs. Penn State. It was the Michigan game.

I have a nephew, D'Shawntae Jones, who's a running back at Glenville and has gotten interest from the Team Up North. When he texted me a picture of him in a Wolverines uniform, I reacted in the only appropriate way: "Fuck you, bitch." I called him and told him I didn't think sending a picture of my flesh and blood in enemy colors was funny. I added that if he did end up going to the Team Up North, I didn't have a problem rooting against him once a year.

Coach Meyer was always intense, but he became even more so during Michigan week. He understood the rivalry from being a grad assistant at Ohio State and growing up in Ashtabula in far northeast Ohio. He understood that losing in The Game got some great coaches fired. He didn't want to fall into that trap. We saw so many times when Michigan had beaten undefeated Ohio State teams and denied us a Big Ten or national championship. We were determined not to let that happen to us.

Unfortunately, our team had something bigger than football, or even the rivalry, on our minds as the Michigan game approached. Earlier that week, Kosta Karageorge, a walk-on defensive lineman, had missed practice. Then another one. He also didn't attend classes. Nobody heard from him or could reach him. Personally, I just thought he was dealing with something and needed time alone. I didn't think the worst at that point.

I'd hung out with Kosta a few times outside the facility, which wasn't the norm for a walk-on, especially one from the other side of the ball. He was just a guy who was full of life, the kind who seemed like he'd give you the shirt off his back. Even though he wasn't on scholarship—his main sport was wrestling, and he was on the OSU team—he was one of the hardest-working dudes on the team. He was always trying to get better. You look at guys who put in extra work after practice, but it just hits you differently when it's a walk-on. Those guys hardly ever play on Saturdays. Kosta didn't. But they work hard not only to make themselves better but to help their teammates get better. There were times on scout team when Kosta would come on to the offensive side and be a fullback just to give the defensive starters a better look. He was just a selfless guy. By Saturday morning, we still hadn't heard anything from or about Kosta. Before the game, they put his picture on the Jumbotron in hopes that someone might come forward with any information about his whereabouts.

With Kosta weighing on our minds, we took the field to play our rivals. The game was tied 14–14 at halftime, and was tied again, at 21, midway through the third quarter. We took the lead on an 81-yard touchdown drive and led 28–21 heading into the fourth quarter.

Then it happened: the moment that changed my career and life. I was about 20 yards behind the line of scrimmage because I liked to watch the defense from the back so I could give J. T. feedback from that perspective to add to the view Coach Herman had from upstairs in the press box. J. T. was tackled near the line of scrimmage. Then I saw the replay on the Jumbotron. He wasn't getting up. I saw them waving the trainers on. *Oh, shit.* This wasn't going to be just one or two handoffs I was going in for, I realized. This was serious. J. T. was like Braxton—he wasn't one of those guys who faked injuries and stayed down so the crowd would get behind him. He had broken his ankle.

> *J. T. Barrett:*
>
> *I tried to get up. I remember tight end Jeff Heuerman came over and looked down and was like, "Oh, snap!" and looked away. Then I looked down and realized, no, I couldn't get up. It wasn't really painful because the adrenaline was popping. It didn't really start banging until later that night. Leaving the field, I was upset and I was hurt, but now let's go win the game. That was all I was worried about.*

I grabbed a ball and put on my helmet and tried to get loose. Other players, including Michigan quarterback Devin Gardner, were consoling J. T. As much as I'd have liked to do that, I had to warm up and get ready to play. The offensive players eventually came to the sideline, where Coach Meyer told us what our next play call would be.

> *Urban Meyer:*
>
> *First of all, your heart is with J. T., just like when Braxton got hurt. And then reality sets in. I remember looking at Cardale, and he had that look on his face like he was getting ready to take a physics exam and he'd never studied physics. I always tell the story about*

> *how I put my arm on his shoulder and said, "You can do this, man. You can do this," and I gave him the play and hit him on the rear end, and he jogged out there, and I was thinking to myself,* There's no way in hell he can do this.

We still had a game to finish. But I could see my teammates' demeanor was just shot. We all kind of hit each other in the helmets to get us back to reality. It didn't go smoothly right away for me. On my first snap, I got stuffed on a third-and-2 run, forcing a punt. My first pass on the next possession was an out cut to the sideline to Mike Thomas. I was so pumped up that it felt like the ball sailed into C-Deck, the top level of the Horseshoe. I then did have an 18-yard run on second-and-15. After a shovel pass to Jalin Marshall, I completed a pass to Corey Smith to set up fourth-and-1 at the Michigan 44. We called timeout with 5:05 left. Coach Meyer decided to go for it instead of punting and called for a handoff to Ezekiel. It wasn't an RPO, but I faked like it was. No doubt respecting my amazing running ability after the 18-yarder, three Michigan defenders followed me and Jalin to the right. Ezekiel slipped a tackle at the line of scrimmage, left tackle Taylor Decker and left guard Billy Price opened a huge gap, and Zeke was gone for the touchdown. On Michigan's next possession, linebacker Darron Lee picked up a fumble caused by Joey Bosa and ran it back for a touchdown to end any doubt about the outcome.

After that game, I had a lot of mixed emotions. The first was that it was a bummer that J. T. had gone down after the season he'd been having. He was our leader, and I knew the opportunities he had to win awards. (He finished fifth in the Heisman Trophy voting even after the injury.) I reached out to J. T. to see how he was doing. He was bummed, even if he tried to downplay it somewhat. I knew his voice when he was down, and his tone told me more than his words.

We didn't really talk about football or our upcoming game in the Big Ten championship. That's not how we operated. We didn't need to speak about the obvious. He didn't need me to tell him to keep his head up. He didn't need to tell me what was at stake the next week.

I was at my apartment that night with a few relatives. I kept my normal routine. No one wanted to mention the elephant in the room: that I was now the guy at quarterback. I remember my uncle Dale asking me how it felt to play in the Game. He expressed his hate for Michigan. You can see in the TV replay of the game that he and a cousin and friends are sitting in the first row of the stands, and a Michigan fan is waving a UM flag and they're slapping it out of his hand. We kept our normal routine after the game. We played video games and watched TV. One thing that I did do differently was that I stayed off social media that night. I didn't want to see the good, bad, or indifferent about what people were saying about not just me but everything. I knew the next day when I went to the Woody, I just wanted to be even more focused than I had been. We had to get ready for the next week. It was like, *Here we go*. I was a little nervous, but I was more eager than anything. I was looking forward to it. I wanted to have the next game right then.

The thrill of beating our rivals didn't last long. During our Sunday practice, police came into the Woody. They talked to Coach Meyer, who then gathered us together. They'd found Kosta. He was dead. He was found in a dumpster near campus with a gunshot wound and a handgun nearby.

Urban Meyer:

There's no training as a coach for that. I got through it with a lot of prayer, and I asked for help. The guys on our team helped me through that too. Defensive tackle Michael Bennett, one of Kosta's close friends, was unbelievable during that time. I knew Kosta and really liked him, but I can't say I was that close with him. He was only on the team for a few months. But he was incredible.

The death was ruled a suicide. At the time, I was skeptical just because he was so upbeat every time we saw him at the Woody. Everyone was like, "How? Why? No way he did that." It's just an example that you never know what someone's going through. A guy like that, so full of life. You felt he'd do anything for you, anything for the team. He had so much more to offer. Why would he take his own life? I definitely wish he'd said something to someone. Any of the guys in our locker room would have done anything and everything in their power to help him get through whatever he was going through. We're more educated about suicide now than we were then. I think he was a prime example of a guy who may have been going through a lot off the field, but when he stepped in the facility, he was all about ball. We try to say that in sports: When you step across those lines, you leave your outside shit at home. I think that's why it took such a toll on so many of us. We were just shocked. This dude was always smiling and laughing and joking with us, and he also did all this extra work busting his butt even though he didn't play in games. You wouldn't have thought there was anything wrong in his life. Looking back and learning what I have about suicide and suicide prevention, it can show itself in many different forms.

A lot of players attended his funeral as a team later in the week while preparing for Wisconsin. Our team had already been through so much: Losing Braxton to injury. Losing to Virginia Tech. Losing J. T. to injury. Now, worst of all, losing Kosta. We were hit with gut-wrenching punches, one after another, almost every week. Now our resilience would be tested again. You couldn't turn on the TV that week without hearing something about Ohio State and how we were going to get hammered by Wisconsin—that I wasn't ready and I'd be the reason why our season was doomed. But one thing I was confident about: me becoming the starting quarterback wasn't going to be an obstacle for us as we went into the postseason.

Chapter 13

PREPARING FOR MY FIRST START

I WOULD LIKE TO THINK my teammates had faith in me heading into the Big Ten Football Championship Game against Wisconsin. They'd seen me in practice all year. They knew what I was capable of. But I hadn't played significant reps in meaningful moments, other than the fourth quarter against the Team Up North. I can only imagine what might have been going on in other guys' minds.

Ever since the Purdue game my freshman year, I had prepared like a starter. But obviously I had more on my plate now. After three years of ups but mostly downs, I would be the starting quarterback for Ohio State. I was all business that week. I loved playing video games, but I put that aside. I studied like never before with Coach Herman at the Woody. I really spent a lot of time on situational football. What do we do if it's third-and-6? What are Wisconsin's tendencies in that situation? What are my options depending on how the play unfolds? I wanted to have everything covered.

Urban Meyer:

I was mesmerized by the transformation that took place instantaneously. I was blown away. I talked to Ted Ginn quite a bit because we had to reach this kid. I needed Ted's help. I needed Michelle's help. And I'm telling you, the day after the Michigan game, he was a different human being. Instantly.

Tyvis Powell:

When he became the starter, that's when I realized something just clicked for him, like he was a totally different guy. I was so used to him playing video games in our apartment. But that week, I remember getting home and he wasn't there. He spent countless hours at the facility. He was with Tom Herman early, late. That boy was locked in. It was great to see.

I think that's mostly overstated. I think Coach Meyer noticed it because before J. T.'s injury, he never really paid attention to me. Of course, I was going to study even harder now that I knew I was the starter. But it's not like I wasn't prepared before. I already had the mentality of preparing like a starter. I don't think people understand how impossible it would be to try to flip a switch and play at an extremely high level if your routine wasn't already established. Can you imagine not studying, not putting extra work in, and trying to do it in four days of practice and get those outcomes? It doesn't work like that. This is major-college football.

Other than freshman Stephen Collier, who hadn't played all year and appeared in only one game in his Ohio State career, we had no other scholarship quarterbacks. But even then, I wasn't sure of my status. I knew I'd start, but Jalin Marshall took plenty of practice reps at quarterback that week. He was a star at that position at Middletown High School in Ohio before switching to receiver at Ohio State. He was an amazing athlete. If he'd played in Ryan Day's offense, he'd be like Jaxon Smith-Njigba—but faster. After J. T. was injured in the Michigan game, Jalin took some wildcat snaps. As we prepared for Wisconsin, Jalin's reps weren't limited to the wildcat. He was getting reps on regular pass plays, not just zone reads or quarterback sneaks. It wasn't like there were two game plans—one for me and one for Jalin.

Urban Meyer:

We practiced with Jalin at quarterback every third series in practice. I had a friend who came to practice, and he looked at me and said, "That's gonna be your quarterback?" We'd run a spread-out pass, and it wouldn't be close to being completed.

I worked closely with Tom Herman all week. Tom was my guy. Our relationship had really gotten better as the season progressed. Even though I'd told him before J. T.'s injury that I intended to transfer after 2014, I think Tom respected how I'd put the team first and stayed ready in case I was needed. He must have thought I needed a confidence booster, though. He had our video guy, Dave Trichel, produce a short highlight tape that included stuff from high school and what I'd done in mop-up duty at Ohio State to help me continue to believe in myself. He said he just wanted to make sure I realized how good I really was. He didn't want me to look at this as an opportunity given to me only because we were stuck with going with me. That was cool, but I didn't need it. I was ready. I remember seeing reports in the media speculating about how much of the offense I knew and whether we'd have to dumb down the playbook for me. I thought that was absurd. I'd been in the system for three years. You think I didn't know the offense?

As for my teammates, they treated me normally. Nobody felt the need to reassure me they had confidence in me. The only thing I remember about that was Zeke saying that in their room, running backs coach Stan Drayton told them they needed to play really well to keep me comfortable. Coaches are supposed to say that. But I was ready. I didn't want to be babied in this game. For me it was, *Let's play football!* Clearly, J. T. and I had different strengths and playing styles, but I just wanted to run our plays.

Tyvis Powell:

Obviously that week was filled with emotions. We just lost J. T. We just lost Kosta. But we used it all as motivation, like, "What would they want us to do? They would want us to play for them and honor them, and the best way to honor them is to try to finish what they started with a ring." Cardale was coming in, and I tweeted something like, "In 12 we trust," with a picture of us smiling after the Team Up North game. "They think you ain't gonna be ready for the Big Ten championship?" It kind of took off. I wasn't worried about Cardale. From the time in high school when I first went up against him, the one thing about Cardale was he could throw that ball.

The only thing that worried me is what I saw in our Tuesday and Wednesday practices. We had walk-ons running the routes. It turned out that our starting receivers weren't used to having to run so much because J. T. tended to underthrow guys on deep routes. But Cardale would throw it 40, 50 yards easy. Our starting receivers' hamstrings were sore from all that running they had to do.

I knew Wisconsin would be a tough challenge. On offense, the Badgers relied on running back Melvin Gordon, who'd already run for 2,260 yards and would finish second in the Heisman Trophy voting. On defense, the Badgers didn't have any huge stars, but they played really well together. They never blew coverages. You never saw that from Wisconsin. Everybody was always in the right position. Did they always have the top athletes? No. But those guys competed at a high level. Wisconsin was second nationally in total defense (260 yards per game) and passing defense (157 yards per game), and fourth in scoring defense (16.8 points allowed per game).

But I was confident. Yes, Wisconsin was statistically very good, but they were in the Big Ten West, which wasn't as strong as the East, which we were in. Even now, a team from the West has never beaten one from the East in the Big Ten Football Championship Game. I knew they weren't as good as the guys we went against every day in practice. If we could do some things against our own guys, I felt confident we could do it against anyone.

Tom Herman:

He was awesome but also nervous as we prepared. Cardale was also juggling quite a bit personally as well. He was a new father and was struggling to keep the peace between his "bio mom" and his "adopted mom." His bio mom began wearing a shirt that said "Cardale's Mom" on the back. At one point, we had to separate their tickets in order to reduce the stress level for Cardale.

> *But Cardale was so happy about the opportunity to play and was willing to put in whatever time he needed to in order to make sure he didn't let his team or his university down. He was a man on a mission, and it was fun for me to be a part of it. We had so many great conversations that week. Not just about football or the game plan but about what he needed to do from a leadership, preparation, and execution standpoint. We really focused on his mindset and his confidence.*

I had so much on my plate at the time. I was a new father and trying to navigate that, especially since Jeaney and I were still learning how to be parents. The ticket issue was another issue I really didn't want to deal with. By that point in my life, I was so beyond worrying about who was in the stands cheering for me. When it counted for me, my momma wasn't at my games when I was a kid or when I was at Ohio State barely playing. Back then, I had all the time in the world on the sideline to look up and see who was there supporting me. Now that I would be starting, I had no time to do that. Michelle was always at my games, but my momma wasn't. In fact, she wasn't even on my regular ticket list. I think we had an allotment of 25 tickets for the Big Ten Football Championship Game, and of course, everyone was asking for them. When you give out your personal allotment, you have to specify each person's relationship to you. I put down Michelle as my mom. That caused a big ruckus when my momma called to get a ticket as my mom. The OSU compliance office told her that Michelle was listed as my mom. That obviously didn't go over well. Very few people knew the details about my personal life and the dynamic among me, Michelle, and my momma, and it was awkward to have to explain. Finally, I just asked if we could separate the 25 who got tickets into different sections in hopes of minimizing any drama.

I just wanted to concentrate on the game. We were a hungry team. Our seniors had never won a ring for either a Big Ten championship or a bowl game. We hadn't won a Big Ten title since 2010, and even that championship was taken away because of the tattoo scandal. The sanctions from that kept us out of the postseason in 2012. And the Michigan State loss in 2013 still stung.

But more was at stake than just a league title this year. It was the first year of the four-team College Football Playoff. After the Virginia Tech game, we were written off. When the first ranking came out, we were 16th. I was thinking we were headed to something like the Alamo Bowl, which was not what we came to Ohio State to play in.

But we gradually moved our way up. After the Michigan game, we were No. 5 behind Alabama, Oregon, TCU, and Florida State. All four of those teams won before our night game against Wisconsin. I didn't think we'd be able to jump any of those teams to get into the playoffs, so my thought was just to worry about ourselves and win the Big Ten championship. Besides, I hadn't been paying attention to the CFP rankings. I didn't understand the voting. I didn't know who picked what. I wasn't thinking about the playoff or any of that stuff. But *everyone* would be by the time we got done that Saturday night.

Chapter 14

59–0!

"Cardale Jones. Cardale Jones. The whole state of Ohio is counting on Cardale Jones."

That's how Fox's Gus Johnson opened the broadcast of the Big Ten title game. That made it seem like the weight of the world was on my shoulders. I didn't really feel that way. I had some nerves, but my mindset was more that I was eager to finally show the world what I could do on a big stage.

Ted Ginn Sr.:

Urban called me the same day J. T. got hurt and he had to put Cardale in the Michigan game. He said, "It looks like he's going to have to be my quarterback." I said, "God blessed you, then." Cardale called me and said he was going to be the starter. I said, "Yep. Now they're really going to see a show." Urban called me back and asked, "Do you really think he can do it?" I told him, "It's been you holding him back. It ain't been him. I said you're going to blow the game if you try to be vanilla. Let the boy throw the ball. He's not going to run all them crazy run plays. He's got receivers. You've got everything. He's going to light it up."

Urban Meyer:

I was very skeptical, but I have a lot of respect for Ted. We didn't necessarily want to do what he suggested until we started seeing Cardale getting in the groove. If he would not have prepared the way he did, we would have handed the ball off to Zeke every time. But I'm telling you that in my coaching career, I've never seen anything like it.

He was the first one in that building, constantly engaged in the game plan. In practice, he was hustling around, leading, earning the respect of his teammates, and earning the respect of his coaches. It was a transformation that in my career, I've never seen anything like that. Never. Not even close.

We were underdogs against Wisconsin. A lot of people forget that. When you win 59–0, it's hard to believe that you weren't supposed to win in a blowout. And that's what it was. Complete domination. We received the opening kickoff. Our first play was a sideline throw on a rollout to Mike Thomas, who made a nice diving catch. Ezekiel Elliott then ran for two first downs. I completed a pass to Corey Smith for another first down to the Wisconsin 38. Tom Herman did a great job of play-calling that settled me down and settled down the whole offense.

Tom Herman:

In simplest terms, the game plan was to hand the ball to Zeke and throw it deep to Devin. With Wisconsin's defensive scheme, we felt like we needed to let Cardale take some shots downfield. He and his teammates executed great.

We didn't waste any time after that cutting loose. I couldn't have had a better target than Devin Smith. After Glenville played Devin's Massillon Washington in high school, we both were on Ohio's Big 33 team that played that All-Star Game against Pennsylvania. We started our chemistry that week, connecting on deep balls a few times. Devin was really fast and was exceptional on deep balls. I haven't been around anyone who was better at tracking long throws. He could make over-the-shoulder catches look routine.

Devin was one of the first people I talked to getting ready for our Sunday practice after the Michigan game. "C'mon, this will be like the Big 33 game," he said. We laughed about it, and then all week we connected on some long throws. We did it again against Wisconsin, which for some reason thought playing man-to-man coverage against our receivers was a good strategy. The Badgers had freshman Sojourn Shelton one-on-one against Devin in the slot. *We've got this*, I thought. *This is about to be big.* It's great when you see a coverage from a defense that you've been working on and know you can beat. You just try not to be too anxious. Devin sprinted downfield and I let the ball go. Devin shielded Shelton from the ball like he was boxing out in basketball and jumped to make the catch. The only issue on the play was that Zeke, who split wide after going in motion, wasn't supposed to go full speed downfield. But he did, and that almost allowed the Badger covering him to have a chance to break up the play. I ran downfield to celebrate with Devin and high-stepped it along the sideline back to the bench, grinning ear to ear. I'd waited my whole career for a moment like this. Even after three years of waiting, it felt like I was riding a bike. But we were just getting started.

We didn't score on our second possession. On third-and-15, I threw deep over the middle to Jalin Marshall into double coverage. If I'd thrown outside to Evan Spencer, I think we'd have had another touchdown.

> *Urban Meyer:*
>
> *Our game plan was not to throw the ball over the middle. When I was a wide receivers coach at Notre Dame, we lost our starting quarterback and our backup was intercepted twice when he threw inaccurately over the middle, and I didn't want the same thing to happen. When Cardale threw that pass into double coverage, I was really upset. But he immediately said, "It's my fault." That was a big deal, because in the past he'd been the kind of guy that blamed others. It was never his fault, and ownership is a big quality of a leader. I actually told him to go tell the offensive line that it was his fault, and he did. That moment galvanized our offense and him as a real starting quarterback in everyone's mind.*

On our next drive, we started at our own 7-yard line, but Zeke ran through a big hole and Wisconsin didn't come close to catching him on an 81-yard touchdown run.

Safety Vonn Bell intercepted a pass to give us the ball back. After I connected with Mike Thomas for 23 yards and Jalin Marshall for 32, we stalled in the red zone and had to settle for a field goal to make it 17–0. Then we put the hammer down at the end of the first half. First, Devin Smith made one of his patented over-the-shoulder grabs for a 44-yard score. Then Zeke capped a 69-yard drive with a 14-yard run to make it 31–0.

The defense provided the capper. Our guys played great all game. The plan was to focus on slowing down Melvin Gordon and make quarterback Joel Stave beat us with his arm. That was not an original strategy. All of Wisconsin's opponents had the same plan that year. We actually succeeded. We frustrated Gordon all night. With the clock winding down in the first half, Wisconsin had the ball at its own 12. Defensive tackle Michael Bennett, who had the honor of wearing Kosta Karageorge's No. 53 that night, knocked the ball out of Gordon's hands. Joey Bosa scooped it up and ran into the end zone to give us a 38–0 lead.

Tyvis Powell:

As a defense that week, we came together. We all believed in Cardale, but let's be real: we were not 100 percent sure how this was going to go. We felt like anybody would be jittery in their first start. So we said that what we needed to do was get him the ball back as much as possible.

The defense was nearly flawless, but our side of the ball wasn't satisfied. At halftime, we were not celebrating. We acted like it was 0–0. Our attitude was simple: Let's go out and finish this thing. We harped on the mistakes we made. We should have had two more touchdowns—one when I threw down the middle and the other when we settled for a field goal.

The blowout continued in the second half. Devin and I hooked up for a 42-yard touchdown when he made another great leaping catch on our first possession. Doran Grant had two interceptions. Wisconsin ran only one play inside our 30-yard line all game, and that play from the 27 ended in a strip-sack by Bennett. Gordon was held to 76 yards in 26 carries. No other Big Ten opponent had held him to fewer than 122 yards. Freshman Curtis Samuel finished off the scoring with two touchdowns. Finally, we were Big Ten champions.

> *Tom Herman:*
>
> *There were a lot of hugs and tears of joy. He thanked me, and I thanked him. I feel there was a ton of mutual appreciation in that moment. It was really special and fulfilling for me and my family to see him shine after three years of hard work and a lot of ups and downs.*

Honestly, it felt like déjà vu. Because even though this was a first, I'd dreamed of a moment like this all my career, all my life, when it came to sports. I had one slip away from me in high school when we lost to Hilliard Davidson in the state finals. *OK,* I thought, *this is what it feels like.* Now I knew that everything we went through and what I went through was worth it—all the ups and downs, all the workouts, everything. It all led to this. All week, and really until we took command after our first few possessions, I still wasn't sure the coaches would stick with me. I truly thought they might use Jalin at quarterback as more than just a change of pace and he could get a significant percentage of the reps. Now I knew I was the unquestioned guy, finally.

We celebrated on the podium. I was named MVP, though I think it should have gone to Zeke, who ran for 220 yards in 20 carries. I had to do the postgame press conference, which I didn't want to do because I wanted to soak in the moment even more with my teammates. By the time I was getting in there, half the team was on the bus.

There would be more opportunities to celebrate.

Chapter 15

WE WANT BAMA

I MIGHT HAVE BEEN the only person in Ohio who didn't spend the rest of that night and the next morning obsessing about whether we'd done enough to make the very first College Football Playoff. All around the country, there was heated debate. Alabama, Oregon, and Florida State were clearly in. TCU was ranked third in the last CFP ranking and had crushed a bad Iowa State team 55–3 early on Saturday. Another Big 12 team, Baylor, was No. 6 and had also won in a blowout. The Big 12 back then didn't have a championship game. We'd made the most of ours, but would the CFP selection committee pick us?

None of this was on my mind. I just figured that our win would ensure a cool bowl game. No Alamo Bowl for us. But I hadn't paid attention to the rankings when they came out every Tuesday. I didn't know how the voting worked and hadn't bothered to learn. That didn't change now. I have to admit that I didn't think they'd have us jump TCU. Besides, I had an infant daughter in Cleveland, so when we got back from Indianapolis, I drove up to see Chloe. I wasn't thinking about our CFP chances. After our win, I got a lot more

Twitter followers, and my phone was blowing up from notifications and phone calls. I was in the process of turning off the notifications when I saw that we were one of the four teams in the CFP and we'd go to New Orleans to play Alabama in the Sugar Bowl in our semi-final. *Wow, that's pretty sweet*, I thought as I realized that's why so many people were calling me. I talked to Coach Meyer. His message: This was a big one, and we had to buckle down.

I spent a couple days in Cleveland. Everybody was talking about our matchup with Alabama and how good Alabama was and how I needed to make sure I was ready. My feeling was that Alabama was a great team, but so were we. This had the potential to be an instant classic. So much would be on the line—the first College Football Playoff, with two of the top programs in the history of college football playing. I don't know how you'd write this up any better even if we had met in the national championship game.

As we began preparation for the Crimson Tide, there was one little hitch. Final exams week followed the Big Ten Football Championship Game, and I hadn't given myself much margin for error. I was taking five classes that semester. I always took the classes that were related to my major—African American and African studies—seriously, but I simply didn't care about some classes outside of my major. I knew what I had to do to stay eligible and on track to graduate. I signed up for one class—I think it was a women's studies class—knowing that I wasn't going to put effort into it. You had to take a certain number of hours, but you only had to pass a certain number of them. Sure enough, I flunked that class. I did well in the two classes related to my major. In the other two, I entered the finals with a borderline C–.

I had developed my own formula academically. I wouldn't worry much about the stuff that didn't count for much of my grades—attendance, homework, pop quizzes. I focused on doing well on exams, which counted for more. That was good enough to get C's, which were sufficient to graduate. But sometimes I cut it close. In these two classes, the final would make or break me. I think I had to get at least an 80 percent on each exam to have them count toward my degree and be eligible for the bowl game. I studied hard for the exams and knew I'd done well. I wasn't worried about my eligibility. But the grades hadn't been posted yet.

One day after practice, we were watching film and I was icing down. Brett Walters, our academic guy, had been bugging me to do extra-credit work for the classes that were shaky. But because I was so confident that I'd done fine on the exams, I refused. I tried to reassure him that I'd get the grades I needed. I busted my butt studying for those exams. Maybe before I was thrust into being a starter, I might not have studied so hard. But I knew the situation I was in and put in the work. Still, I was young and dumb and stubborn. Why do extra work when I wouldn't need it?

But Brett was concerned enough that he interrupted our film session to deliver news that I'm sure he dreaded giving to Coach Meyer. He told him that I probably wouldn't be eligible for the Alabama game. Oh, boy. I'd told Brett a thousand times, "Calm down," when he pestered me about the extra credit. I told him I'd done well on the exams. But the grades weren't in yet. This was a Tuesday, and I think the grades would be posted that Friday. Brett explained to Coach Meyer how we had gotten to this point. Coach Meyer pulled him out of the meeting room and just ripped him: "How did we let our athletes slip behind like this, if it's true? And how is it this is the first time I'm hearing about this?" Brett was about to cry—a grown-ass man about to cry. He was flustered and was telling Coach Meyer that I'd recently been picking it up on those classes and that I wouldn't listen to him about doing extra credit. Coach Meyer said to Brett, "So you're saying there's a chance we aren't going to have a quarterback for this Alabama game?" I think what really got to Coach Meyer was when I turned to Brett and said,

"I told you at the beginning of the semester I don't do homework. Don't act like it's a surprise to you. If you haven't been relaying that message to Coach or I'm going to get punished for that, that's not on me." Coach Meyer finally turned to me and asked if I had done well enough on the exams. I told him yes.

> *Urban Meyer:*
>
> *It was right before Christmas, and I got a knock on the door. The academic guy knocked on the frickin' door of the game-plan meeting. You don't ever do that, you know? It better be serious. I looked up, and someone said, "It's Brett, and he wants to talk to you." I said, "What? What do you mean? We're busy here." I walked out there and he said we might have a problem with Cardale. I said, "A problem with Cardale?" He kind of told me what was going on, and I made make sure everyone was alerted because we didn't have a bona fide backup quarterback.*
>
> *It was devastation. But after I talked to Brett, I kind of knew that he was gonna be all right. But one of the biggest worries was if something happened to Cardale. We were playing in the College Football Playoff, and my backup quarterback was a wishbone high school quarterback.*

I was right. I aced the finals and ended up with B's in both of those classes. I'm not sure Brett has ever forgiven me for putting him through that, though. To this day, I give him shit about it. "Urban was about to make you cry," I tell him mockingly.

My academic status wasn't the only issue I faced heading into the Alabama game. Before we left for New Orleans, I went back home to see family, including one last visit with my beloved uncle Audi. I'd always been close to him and my other uncles. They'd served as father figures for me. Uncle Audi had always been so full of life. To me, he was the definition of what a man should be. He'd been diagnosed with cancer. He was a man of faith, and that gave him optimism he could beat it. But the cancer he had was terminal, and he'd entered hospice care. I'd last seen him in the summer, and now he looked completely different. He was skin and bones and couldn't really talk. It was extremely hard to see him that way. (He died a few days after the Alabama game, which I heard he watched. I'm so glad that I was able to provide him with a thrill in his final days.)

Uncle Audi was on my mind as we prepared for the game. I was sad about him, but I was angry at Tom Herman. Our relationship had come a long way from our rough early start. As I've said before, because of my upbringing I struggled with trusting people and allowing myself to feel vulnerable. I had just been hurt too much in the past when I'd let my guard down; it was easier to have a certain detachment. But Coach Herman and I had really developed a close relationship as the 2014 season went on. I had earned his trust by being more diligent about doing the small things. I'd gotten better at "playing the game" to keep him and others off my ass. That led them to giving me more leeway. I was treated more like an adult. During pregame warm-ups before the Indiana game late in the year, I was joking with Coach Herman. "I remember when I couldn't stand you," I said. "I was gonna whup your ass." We were laughing about it. He said, "No, Dale, you changed." Maybe he was right. Heading into the postseason, we were in sync.

Then Coach Herman started to be mentioned as a head coach candidate for other jobs. As he should have been. He deserved it after the success we'd had in his two years at Ohio State. Rumors spread that he was going to take the job at Houston. The quarterbacks and Coach Herman had a private group chat, and I posted something like, "Oh, man. This is sweet. You're getting a new job." He replied, "Oh, no. I'm all in."

I interpreted that to mean that he was going to stay at Ohio State. Then a couple of weeks before the Alabama game, he was announced as Houston's head coach. That he would stay with us until the end of the season wasn't much consolation. I was like, *The motherfucker just lied to us.* I think I sent him a screenshot with the news of his hiring on it, and wrote something like, "I thought you weren't taking the job."

The quarterbacks had a separate group chat that didn't include coaches, and we were like, "Fuck that dude. The motherfucker wants to leave us, wants to lie to us." I wasn't upset he was leaving. Everyone knew he wanted to be a head coach. I wanted him to have success and have this opportunity. But him saying he was all in and then leaving bothered me. Just after I'd dropped my guard, I'd gotten burned again. I thought about the times when being honest to a fault hurt me. When I'd gotten in trouble for doing things such as missing a tutoring session, I hadn't lied. I'd just told the truth. I said I was tired or simply didn't want to. Then I'd paid the price.

Coach Herman tried to defend himself. He said he wanted to keep the focus on the game and not have his departure be a distraction. But still, in my view, he had lied. I wasn't in a forgiving mood. So as the Alabama game approached, we didn't speak. When I had no choice but to communicate with him, I was dry as hell. Our relationship didn't thaw as we got to New Orleans. During pregame warm-ups, I tried to avoid him. During the game, I spent as little time as possible on my headset with him. After drives, I'd take as much time as I could drinking water and Gatorade and finding ways to avoid communicating directly with him up in the booth. I don't really think it affected my performance in the game. Most of the communication on the headset is about routine stuff: "What did you see on this play?" "We're probably going to start the drive with this." "Be alert for this or that." I could do that with others or have someone else act as a go-between. Still, it's not the kind of situation you want to have between a quarterback and his position coach/offensive coordinator.

Tom Herman:

I don't remember not being on "speaking terms," although he was a bit distant. My intent was not to deceive him about the Houston job but instead to downplay it so it wasn't a distraction. We certainly talked throughout the preparation for the game. I know now that he was upset then, but like a true pro and a great family member, I think he thought it would be best to talk about it after the dust settled. And he knew we had a job to do together.

Nobody outside the program knew about the frost between me and Coach Herman. But even without that knowledge, not many people gave us a chance against No. 1 Alabama. The Crimson Tide's only loss came in a 23–17 defeat by Ole Miss in early October. They had a few close calls, but they'd crushed Missouri 42–13 in the SEC Championship Game.

Alabama was an amazing team. The Tide had studs on defense such as Landon Collins, Trey DePriest, Reggie Ragland, A'Shawn Robinson, and Cyrus Jones. As always with a Nick Saban–coached team, they were rarely out of position. On offense they had wide receiver Amari Cooper, who finished third in the Heisman voting.

Running backs T. J. Yeldon and Derrick Henry, the latter of whom would win the Heisman in 2015 and become an NFL star, shared the ball; each had run for 11 touchdowns and almost reached 1,000 yards. O. J. Howard was a dangerous tight end. Blake Sims, who'd waited his entire career to be a starter, could run as well as throw.

Alabama didn't have many weaknesses, but the Crimson Tide gave us motivation with some of their comments leading up to the game. I think Collins said our semifinal would be like a warm-up for them before the national championship game. On media day, they said some similar things. It just showed us what everyone thought, that they didn't respect us. That gave me a bigger chip on my shoulder. We heard all about the SEC's dominance over Ohio State and the Big Ten. The only time we'd beaten an SEC team was a Sugar Bowl win in the 2010 season over Arkansas, which was vacated because of the tattoo scandal. So officially we had never beaten an SEC team. We heard the same old stuff about us not being as fast as they were. We wanted to be the team that changed that perception.

Ted Ginn Sr.:

After the Wisconsin game, Urban called me about the next game. He was scared to death of Alabama. He asked me what I thought. I told him he couldn't be scared to throw the ball: "You've got a pistolero there, bro. Let him throw it." I talked to him during the week, and he said, "Will you come down and sit down with Cardale?" I said, "Urban, he's good."

I went down and went to practice. Cardale is so confident in what he does, and he's always smiling, so you don't believe he knows what he's doing. He doesn't show that nervousness. The team practiced that day in helmets and shorts only, but Cardale came out with helmet and shoulder pads. That concerned Urban. I had to tell him that Cardale wanted to wear shoulder pads because he didn't want to mess up his timing.

The game was played in New Orleans. That's SEC territory. I remember hearing from not just my family but other people's families that Alabama fans were nasty to them. They were cocky, saying they were getting ready to go to Dallas for the national championship game after this little pit stop. The Rose Bowl between Oregon and Florida State in the other CFP semifinal was the game before ours. On the pregame shows, everyone picked Alabama to crush us. We were underdogs by more than a touchdown.

Urban Meyer:

We had a really good offensive line and a really good defensive line. I've been in enough championship games to know that if you can control the line of scrimmage, that solves a lot of shortcomings anywhere else because everywhere else, if you get to that point, usually they're good. But just like the rivalry game, whoever wins the line of scrimmage is going to win the game. And I really felt good about our offensive and defensive lines, and then we had to be really smart with Cardale.

We were about to shock the world. From the start, we showed we could play with Bama. We forced a three-and-out on their first possession when cornerback Doran Grant broke up a third-down pass to Cooper. On our first series, I ran for a first down on third down after Evan Spencer almost made an incredible one-handed catch the previous play. Jalin Marshall ran for another first down.

We wanted to use tempo and wide runs to tire out their big, talented defensive linemen. We knew running straight at Alabama probably wouldn't work consistently. On second-and-13, Zeke took a handoff and ran toward the right sideline. It didn't look like much was there, but he turned the corner and hurdled a stumbling Bama defender for a 54-yard gain to the Alabama 5.

Just as I had a chip on my shoulder for that game, so did Zeke. Before the game, Pro Football Hall of Fame running back Emmitt Smith said that there were two great running backs playing in the Sugar Bowl and that both played for Bama—Yeldon and Henry. At that point in his career, Zeke was a bit of an unknown. He played with a broken wrist all year, one sign of his toughness. The second half of the season, he really came on to be a guy who we all know of now. I've played with guys who I'd rather have the ball than Zeke. But Zeke is probably the best player I've ever played with on offense because of his football IQ and the fact that he played just as hard without the ball. But he was also damn good with the ball in his hands, as he showed that postseason.

With the ball at the 5, we should have punched it in. But we couldn't. On third down, I had to throw the ball away under pressure, and we settled for a field goal by Sean Nuernberger. Most of the rest of the first half was just as frustrating. Zeke got the ball punched out from him, and Alabama capitalized on a touchdown run by Henry. On the possession after that, Devin Smith caught another deep ball and we had first-and-goal at the 1. The next play was supposed to be a jump pass. But I took my eye off the ball and it bounced off my helmet. I caught it and tried to scramble but was tackled at the 9. If I'd caught it, Evan would have been wide open in the end zone. Once again, we settled for a field goal.

Alabama then had a long drive for a touchdown. We were trying to answer. We'd gotten a first down and called for a hitch pattern to Devin. But instead of stopping, he kept running. My pass was intercepted by Cyrus Jones, who returned it all the way to our 15. Alabama converted a fourth-and-1 at the 5 before Yeldon scored to make it 21–6. We'd been outplaying Bama, but our mistakes were killing us. Twice we'd stalled inside their 10 and had that stupid miscommunication with Devin.

When Alabama starts pulling away, it's rare that an opponent rallies. But we knew we could play with them. We didn't get flustered. On our next possession, I completed a pair of 26-yard passes to Jalin Marshall on third-and-long, and Zeke scored on a three-yard carry. Then our defense forced a three-and-out, giving us the ball at our 23 with 1:24 left. A couple of first downs moved it to the Bama 40. On the next play, I dropped back to pass but didn't see anyone open. I took off up the middle and shed a couple of tackles. Right in front of me was Landon Collins. I hadn't forgotten his comment about us being a warm-up for the national championship. When I got in the open field, I was looking for him. *Where is No. 26? Where is No. 26?* No way was I going to slide to avoid contact or even try to evade him. I lowered my shoulder and plowed him. "Get up, bitch," I told him when we got up. "We ain't done with y'all yet."

No, we weren't. Two plays later, we called for a trick play. I handed off to Jalin, who flipped the ball to Evan Spencer. We'd called this play in the Michigan State game, but Evan Spencer didn't like what he saw and tucked it. He was determined to throw it this time. Alabama wasn't fooled. Cyrus Jones had Mike Thomas well covered. But Evan's pass was perfect. It sailed just over Jones's hands, and Mike made an unbelievable catch, leaping high and somehow keeping his left foot inbounds with momentum carrying him out of bounds. It's a game of inches, right?

Tom Herman:

When we talked about the reverse pass from Evan Spencer to Michael Thomas in between series, Cardale did not want me to call that play. I believe he said something along the lines of, "Coach, we don't need to run a gadget play to beat these guys." That made me laugh over the headset. I said to him, "Spoken like a true QB. The great ones always want the ball in their hands." A pretty cool exchange during a huge game.

It was the kind of play that Mike worked so hard to make. Even though we were roommates at Fork Union, I wouldn't say we became close friends. Even at Ohio State, our paths were kind of similar. He played as a freshman but struggled early in his sophomore year and redshirted in 2013. That's a rare thing to happen, and he took it personally. He changed his body. He changed his eating habits. He changed his mentality. Every day, he attacked practice. He was a perfectionist. He wanted to be the best. His uncle is Keyshawn Johnson, who was once the top pick in the NFL Draft and had a very good NFL career. Mike was a second-round pick by New Orleans and became one of the best receivers in the NFL, if not the best. I'm not sure any play he has made in the pros was as amazing as the one against Alabama, though, or as important. We went to halftime down 21–20, but it felt like we were ahead.

Soon enough, we would be. We got the ball first in the second half. After a couple of completions to Mike, we had third-and-8 at the Alabama 47. Time to dial up Devin. As I waited for him to get downfield, the Bama pass rush almost got to me. Just as I let the ball go, linebacker Xzavier Dickson grabbed my face mask. Because of that, I couldn't get everything on the ball and underthrew it. But Eddie Jackson, the guy covering Devin in man-to-man, tripped. Evan made the easy catch for a 47-yard touchdown. I'm sure our fans panicked when they saw a penalty flag in our backfield. That's usually holding, but I knew it was for the face mask. We were ahead 27–21.

It stayed that way until late in the third quarter. Then defensive end Steve Miller made the biggest defensive play of the game. Steve is from Canton, and we were teammates in the Big 33 game and became friends. In practice for the Alabama game, I watched as we installed a defensive play in which Steve dropped back in coverage like a linebacker. I was like, *What is Steve doing dropping back?* Steve would tell you that Luke Fickell told him, "They're going to throw it right to you, big fella." I remember when they asked Stephen Collier, our scout-team quarterback, to throw it to Steve in practice, he didn't want to do it. Quarterbacks hate to throw interceptions, even on purpose. But he complied, something I probably wouldn't have done if I'd been the scout-team quarterback.

But our coaches obviously saw something on Alabama tape that they thought they could exploit. That's why coaches coach and players play. Now it was time to use it. Miller lined up in his normal spot, took a step forward as if to pass-rush, and then dropped back. Sims clearly didn't notice him. He threw toward Cooper, who ran a slant. But Miller was right in front of him. He made the catch and got a block from Doran Grant early and Curtis Grant late for a 41-yard pick-six and a 34–21 lead.

Just when it looked like we were in command, Alabama came alive. Henry took a short pass and turned it into a 52-yard gain, and Sims scored on a short carry. Alabama had a chance to retake the lead after our punt took a horrible bounce and was downed at our 23 with about 10 minutes left. But then safety Vonn Bell made a huge play. Bell was a five-star recruit signed right out of SEC country. It was a signal that Coach Meyer was going to go toe-to-toe with the Alabamas of the world for the top talent, no matter where it was. Vonn, who helped the Cincinnati Bengals get to the Super

Bowl in 2022 with an overtime interception against Kansas City in the AFC Championship Game, was an ultra-confident player. He talked about opening the Vonn Bell Academy to teach defense when his playing days ended. "VBA," he'd say. "VBA, 24 hours a day." If the Kansas City interception will be Exhibit A at VBA, his play against Alabama will be next. He baited Sims into thinking tight end O. J. Howard was open, and then dashed in front of Howard for an interception to keep us ahead.

We traded punts on our next two possessions—Coach Meyer tossed his headset because he thought Alabama should have been called for roughing Cam Johnston on ours—before we got the ball at our own 5 with 5:20 left. After I ran for five yards, we faced a third-and-1. We hadn't had a first down since midway through the third quarter after failing to convert our last four third downs. The call was a keeper. Collins hit me behind the line, but I spun and was able to fall backward for the first down. As I hit the turf, defensive back Nick Perry hit me in the back of the helmet. All three of us were slow to get up. In my case, I know why. I'm pretty sure I was concussed. When I got up, I was so messed up that I looked to the Alabama sideline for the play call. But there was no way I was coming out of that game.

Our next play was a handoff to Zeke. I was supposed to signal to Evan Spencer to go in motion so he could block. I remember thinking, *Man, there's something I'm supposed to do with him*. But in my fuzzy state, I thought, *Fuck it. Set. Go*. Somehow Evan got where he needed to be anyway. He blocked three guys like they were bowling pins, and that sprung Zeke for his famous Run through the Heart of the South 85-yard touchdown for a 42–28 lead. I still joke with Evan that I did that on purpose, that if he'd gone in motion, Alabama would had adjusted its defense and Zeke's run might not have happened.

We went for the two-point conversion after the score. My concussion was still affecting me. I threw to Corey Smith, but it was a horrible pass. Fortunately, Mike Thomas was there to make the catch.

Alabama made it interesting by scoring a quick touchdown and had a chance for a miracle in the final minute before Tyvis intercepted Sims's Hail Mary to clinch our 42–35 win.

For our program and our fans, it was the sweetest of wins. We'd beaten the kings of the supposedly unbeatable SEC. I didn't get caught up in that. To me, the victory just meant we'd play for the national title. Alabama was an unbelievable team, but that wasn't our championship game. Our goal wasn't just to beat Bama. They were just in our path to get to our ultimate goal.

Chapter 16

WINNING IT ALL

We were now in uncharted territory. For the entire history of college football, the season ended with a bowl game. With the arrival the College Football Playoff, there'd be one more game, and it was for everything. In the first CFP championship game, we'd be playing Oregon at AT&T Stadium near Dallas, Texas. I had thought defending champion Florida State, with 2011 Heisman Trophy–winning quarterback Jameis Winston, would beat the Ducks. But Oregon crushed the undefeated Seminoles 59–20 in their semifinal at the Rose Bowl, ending Florida State's 29-game winning streak. It had been a tight game at halftime, with the Ducks narrowly leading 18–13. Then Oregon scored six touchdowns in fewer than 17 minutes to blow it open.

When Coach Meyer was informed of the final score in our post-game press conference, he jokingly popped out of his chair as if he had to bolt to start preparation immediately. Oregon posed several challenges. For one, their quarterback, Marcus Mariota, had just won the Heisman Trophy. Entering the title game, he'd thrown for 4,121 yards and 40 touchdowns with only 3 interceptions. He'd also run for more than 700 yards and 15 touchdowns. With plenty of playmakers around him who excelled in open space, he'd be quite the challenge for our defense.

Much was made of the fact that Oregon had a Heisman winner at quarterback and Ohio State had a third-stringer. It didn't matter to me. I was a fan of Mariota. He was a great player. But he wouldn't be on the field at the same time as me. I would face Oregon's defense, not Mariota. I never felt, no matter who the opposing quarterback was, that I had to outdo him. I always considered it my job to stay within the game plan and our system and put our team in the best position to have success.

But we did think it would be a shootout. Oregon hadn't scored fewer than 42 points since its only loss, 31–24 at home to Arizona in early October. The Ducks had won every game after that by at least 12 points and usually a lot more. Much of Oregon's success came from their tempo. Their goal was to run a play every 16 seconds. That crazy pace gave defenses no chance to catch their breath. All over the Woody, we had 16 signs as constant reminders of our task.

Oregon's defense didn't get the same attention as its offense, but it was pretty good too. The Ducks hadn't allowed more than 20 points in any of their previous 4 games. They had forced 30 turnovers—18 fumbles and 12 interceptions—and led the country in turnover margin at plus-20. Defensive tackle DeForest Buckner and defensive end Arik Armstead—who would both go on to lengthy NFL careers—anchored the line. Derrick Malone and Joe Walker were quality linebackers. Safety Erick Dargan had seven of Oregon's interceptions.

We were six-point underdogs. That didn't matter to us. Our confidence level was sky-high. After crushing Wisconsin and beating Alabama, we didn't care what opponent was in front of us. You never got the vibe throughout that season that we were going to lose. Our feeling was that if we stuck together—and we would—we had this. After our postseason wins, we were ready to take on anybody.

My confidence level personally was through the roof, but it was as much because of my teammates as my own performance. I don't think I played as well as the media portrayed it. Against Wisconsin, I made errors that cost us maybe two touchdowns. (Imagine the final score if I hadn't.) Against Alabama, I had the interception and some other plays I'd like to have a chance to do over. After every game, coaches would pore over the film and grade each player. The standard for excellence was to be graded as a "champion." I didn't achieve that in either the Wisconsin or Alabama game because of my mistakes. So while I was confident, I also knew I hadn't played anywhere near my own potential. I was looking for another opportunity to try to do that.

We got to Texas and got a warm reception. We have a huge fan base down there, particularly in Dallas, and they gave us a lot of support in the few days we were there. But it also could be a bit much. Everyone wanted a piece of us.

Michelle Nash:

The day before the game, we were at the Ohio State team hotel and heard that some little kids wanted to see Cardale. He didn't want to go downstairs because he'd probably get mobbed. He asked where they were, and we told him they were on the first floor. Cardale got a bunch of footballs and signed them and then threw them to the boys from the balcony on the second floor. They threw one back up to him, and then Cardale told them to run little pass routes and he tossed it to them. He stayed there for about a good half hour talking to them and throwing them the ball. That just warmed my heart.

That was a nice diversion, but I mostly tried to eliminate distractions. I blocked almost all the contacts on my phone except for Michelle and Tom Herman because I wanted to concentrate on my preparation without having my phone constantly dinging. When we got to the stadium, which is nicknamed Jerry's World after Dallas Cowboys owner Jerry Jones, we were blown away. It was pretty new, and everything was over-the-top. The Jumbotron, which stretched over most of the length of the field, was amazing. The stadium's seating capacity is about 80,000, which is more than 20,000 less than the Shoe, but it looked huge. No way did it seem possible that it could be packed. But it would be—mostly with Ohio State fans.

When game day arrived, I was excited for the game, of course. But I also was excited to see what uniforms Oregon would wear. Nike is headquartered in Oregon, and Phil Knight is a huge supporter of the program. One of its signatures is that they wear different uniforms every game. Oregon wore light uniforms and helmets with dark numbers. Pretty cool, but I have to say, I was a little disappointed.

I was more disappointed with our start. Oregon got the opening kickoff and went right through our defense. The Ducks didn't even need a third-down conversion to go 75 yards in 11 plays for a touchdown. The only trouble they faced on the drive was when running back Thomas Tyner fumbled the ball. But it bounced right back to him like he was a basketball player dribbling. That's when I thought, *Oh my God, everything is going their way right now.* You've got to be careful when stuff like this happens.

Tyvis Powell:

Going into the Oregon game, we were feeling like the Alabama game should have been the championship game. [The Oregon game] felt like a regular Saturday game, even though it was Monday night. That was the attitude going into the game. Obviously, Oregon switched that up with that first drive real quick.

On the sideline, we had one thought: *Now it's our turn to answer.* But we didn't. I ran for one first down on third down but was tackled short of the marker on the next third down.

We started our next possession at our 3-yard line after an Oregon punt was downed there. On second down, I dropped back to pass in the end zone and threw the ball away after sidestepping a sack that would have been a safety. On the next play, the offensive line gave me great protection, which allowed Corey Smith to get open for a 26-yard gain.

That lit the fuse. After that, we were pretty unstoppable—except when we stopped ourselves. On the next play, I threw to Jalin Marshall, who made an unbelievable catch, trapping the ball off the defender's back, for another 26-yard gain. Honestly, I should have thrown to tight end Nick Vannett, who was wide open underneath. We then faced a fourth-and-2 at the Oregon 35. Jalin barely got the first down on a shovel pass to keep the drive alive. Zeke then found a hole and weaved for a 33-yard touchdown to tie the game.

We caught a huge break on Oregon's next possession. On third-and-long, Mariota threw deep to a wide-open receiver, who dropped the ball. We got the ball on a short field after a nice punt return by Jalin and went to work again. After a completion for a first down to Mike Thomas, I threw into the end zone for Devin Smith, who drew an interference call. Zeke ran through a big hole opened by our line to set up a one-yard TD pass to Nick. I bobbled the snap on the touchdown and was afraid I'd be late on the pass, but thank God he caught it.

At this point, we knew our offensive line had taken control. Collectively those guys, nicknamed the Slobs, were unbelievable. They were like a family within our bigger Buckeyes family. They always hung out together. They always ate together. They held each other accountable and took pride in being the heart and soul of our offense. Everything ran through them, whether it was protecting the quarterback or opening holes in the run game.

They were the backbone to our success. I think Zeke rushed for more than 700 yards in those three postseason games. You could drive a truck through some of those holes. Clearly Zeke took a lot of those runs the distance. But it's a running back's dream to have offensive linemen handling the four guys up front and getting to the second level, and the first guy you've got to beat is a safety 12 yards down the field and you're in space. Our line was the heart and soul of our team. Everybody gave me a lot of credit for what we did. Compared to them, I did nothing.

Each lineman had his own distinct personality. Left tackle Taylor Decker had the most experience. He started on the undefeated 2012 team at right tackle before shifting to the left side in 2014. He was the guy everyone looked up to and who really embraced protecting the quarterback's blind side. He was one of Ohio State's five first-round picks in the 2016 NFL Draft.

Left guard Billy Price, who started his career as a defensive lineman, was the youngest and newest player on the line. But he was by far the most athletic, and even challenged me to throwing competitions. He had a cannon—he could throw 60 yards easily—but fell short in our long-toss competitions. Billy became a first-round pick by the Bengals.

Center Jacoby Boren and right guard Pat Elflein were the jokesters. They were sarcastic as hell and the life of the party. Both guys are guys you wanted in your corner when shit hit the fan. Pat was a third-round pick by Minnesota in the 2017 NFL Draft. Both Pat and Billy would win the Rimington Trophy as college football's best center after moving to that position later in their OSU careers.

Jacoby wasn't as talented as those guys, but he made up for it with toughness. He had little, fat, stubby ankles that were always getting rolled up on. But he played through it. That happened to him against Alabama pretty bad, and I thought he was freaking done. But he only missed one play. Chase Farris came in, Billy moved to center, and we ran a play behind them on Zeke's three-yard touchdown run. That we would run a play behind two guys playing their first play at new positions showed the confidence our coaches had in those guys.

Darryl Baldwin was the right tackle. Like Billy, he was a converted defensive lineman. He might have been the oldest guy on the team. We called him Uncle D. But that wasn't just because of his age. It was because he just could not bend, even though he was really an athletic guy. He always looked like he had a tight back. But he filled a big hole at right tackle.

Back to the game. We were up 14–7 and rolling. But we were our own worst enemy. On our next possession, we were driving when I botched a handoff with Zeke and Oregon recovered the fumble. It was an RPO, and I was going to throw it, but Oregon played it well. So I was going to give it to Zeke, but I hit his elbow and the ball came free. That was definitely my fault. It was devastating because it was self-inflicted. The consolation was that we knew they couldn't stop us if we could get out of our own way.

Fortunately, our defense answered the challenge when the Ducks got close to scoring. On fourth-and-goal from the 3, Tyvis led the charge in filling the hole and stopping Thomas Tyner just short of the goal line. We drove again, with Zeke getting 26 yards to give us some breathing room. I then found Corey Smith open deep. It looked like a potential touchdown, but Oregon's Troy Hill lowered his helmet and knocked the ball from Corey's grip, and the Ducks recovered the fumble at their 10. Corey had good ball security. It was just a perfect play by Hill. Still, it was two straight drives that could have been touchdowns that ended with nothing.

We wouldn't be denied the next time. Our defense continued to dominate, forcing a three-and-out. On third-and-12, I stepped up in the pocket after getting a little pressure. I saw Devin Smith open downfield. If I'd thrown it farther, he probably would have scored. But he made the catch at the 6 for a 45-yard gain. I ran it the next three plays and scored on a one-yard run to make it 21–7. Oregon drove for a field goal to make it 21–10 at halftime.

We had a chance to extend the lead at the start of the third quarter. On fourth-and-1 at the Oregon 33, we called for a quarterback sneak up the middle. They put Buckner and Armstead, their two best and biggest linemen, right over Jacoby, with two linebackers right behind them. I knew there was no way we were converting that up the middle, so I bounced it outside to the left, going back to the 40 to escape a tackler. I then dove over a defensive back for a first down. I might not have been a runner like J. T. or Braxton, but I could run it when I had to.

But on the very next play, Jalin had the ball bounce out of his hands to an Oregon defender for an interception. We knew Oregon's defense was based on turnovers, and they were in position for every little mistake we made. The Ducks took advantage. Mariota threw over the middle to Byron Marshall, who outran our DBs for a 70-yard touchdown. It was now 21–17. This game wasn't over.

Then I made it worse. On our next possession, I rolled out when Oregon pressured me. I was trying to throw the ball away when the ball slipped out of my hand. That might have been one time when not gripping the ball with the laces cost me. Oregon recovered at our 23 and moved to our 6. Mariota threw a perfect pass over our defender to tight end Evan Baylis in the back of the end zone. Baylis jumped and caught the ball, but our cornerback Eli Apple pushed him out of the end zone before he could get a foot down. Instead of a touchdown, it was an incompletion. What a huge play. Oregon kicked a field goal, but we still had the lead.

It was a moment of truth for us. After all we'd been through, we were letting it slip away. That had to stop, and it did. We drove 75 yards for a touchdown. Mike Thomas had a 17-yard reception. I plowed the Oregon nose tackle to pick up a first down on third-and-3. But mostly it was Zeke and our offensive line. He ran for 44 yards on the drive, including 11 and 9 on the last two plays, to put us up 28–20 at the end of the third quarter.

We could see Oregon's defense was tired. Our linemen were just wearing them out with their physicality. On the sideline, everyone, including me, told our coaches to keep pounding the ball on the ground. Zeke was in a rhythm, with Curtis Samuel an effective change of pace. So that's mostly what we did. I threw to Mike Thomas, who made a nice sideline move to get at least an extra 10 yards, and then to Jalin to the 10. Zeke again did the rest to make it 35–20.

By then our defense had taken control too. Even more than anything we were doing on offense, that made me feel confident that we had this. Oregon had us on our heels early with their tempo, but our guys had settled in. We were triggering and playing aggressively with their hands and changing the line of scrimmage. I was like, *Man, we're good.*

Oregon would need Mariota to create some magic if we were going to be threatened. Joey Bosa made sure that didn't happen. He hit Mariota and drove him to the ground on his right (throwing) shoulder just after the quarterback threw. Honestly, if this were an NFL game, Joey probably would have been fined $75,000. Oregon's offensive linemen were pissed and started jawing with Joey. One of them, Jake Fisher, obviously said too much because he was called for unsportsmanlike conduct. With seldom-used backup Jeff Lockie in, the Ducks had no chance. They didn't get a first down and had to punt.

We went three-and-out, and Mariota showed guts by returning. But our defense was too good. On fourth-and-11 Mariota threw high to his receiver, who got hit by Tyvis for an incompletion that ended any doubt about the outcome. We punched in a final score with Zeke scoring his fourth touchdown with 28 seconds left to put us ahead 42–20. As I went to the sideline, I saw LeBron James and former players such as Carlos Hyde and Bradley Roby. Seeing those guys and how happy they were for us was pretty cool. Coach Meyer and I hugged. The same with me and our offensive linemen. Backup lineman Antonio Underwood, who was also from Cleveland, had his back turned to me, and I jumped on it.

We'd done it. We were national champions. It was such a great feeling. Everything we'd done to get to this point was worth it. My favorite part of the postgame celebration was getting a team picture taken on the field after the postgame press conference. This was a championship that would bond us together, and the picture was a perfect way to capture the moment. I'll remember it forever. As we celebrated, I remembered how different everything had been just weeks earlier. J. T. had established himself as the quarterback. He was a year younger than me, so I would have had to transfer if I were going to be a starting college quarterback. Now I was a national champion after just three starts. It was just a surreal feeling.

Sheena Jones:

I had tears of joy. I was there front and center for the last three games. I went to a lot of the games, even the ones he didn't play in. When they won it, I was just so happy. I knew he could do it. I remember when Cardale was playing Pop Warner and Ted Ginn Jr.

and Troy Smith first made it to the NFL. He was like, "I want to be like them." I said, "You can do whatever you want to do." And he did.

When I finally got to the locker room, it was clear my teammates had a helluva party in there while I was doing interviews. I missed a great celebration. I even missed a chance to sing our fight song afterward. As the equipment guys packed up our stuff and most of the team was on the bus, I checked my phone. I had at least 400 messages. I talked with Coach Herman on the bus ride back to the hotel, and we patched things up. He would be headed to Houston to start his new job, and I'm glad he left with us on good terms.

Tom Herman:

Winning the championship was life-changing, something I'll remember vividly for the rest of my life. I was so happy and proud for the guys in that QB room. Braxton set the foundation with his phenomenal play for two seasons. Then J. T. took us all the way to the championship game as a redshirt freshman. Then Cardale came in to the three biggest games of the year and was unfazed by the magnitude of the situation. It was a surreal journey, and I can't thank those QBs enough for making it memorable.

We still talk often to this day. I just had no idea how much I'd miss him the next year.

Chapter 17

A DECISION TO MAKE

We celebrated all night. We didn't get back to the team hotel until about 1:00 or 2:00 AM. I got dressed up and went with some teammates and former Buckeyes for a night on the town. We went to a strip club—the first and only time I've ever been to one. Someone handed me a wad of one-dollar bills—400 of them. It was the most money I'd ever seen in my life. As we partook in the scenery, I was such a novice that I didn't know what I was supposed to do with the dollar bills. OK, I did know; I'm not that naive. But was I supposed to throw them? *No way*, I thought. I put almost all but about $20 of it in the pocket of my hoodie and zipped it up. After we got back home, I went to Cleveland and deposited the money in the bank. I have to admit it was kind of embarrassing to deposit almost $400 in single dollar bills.

Urban Meyer:

I didn't know about the strip club. He didn't share that with me, which is fine.

That night was surreal. When we finally left the club, it was light outside. I was like, *What just happened?* I was still high from the thrill of the game. When we got to the hotel, I looked at my phone and saw I had text messages saying that the bus for that morning's traditional press conference for the national champions was leaving soon. I went to my room and changed into some Ohio State gear and got on the bus. Tyvis and I joined Coach Meyer for the traditional press conference for the national champions. Tyvis had been named the game's defensive MVP.

Urban Meyer:

What I remember about that morning was a talk we had. One of our big sayings that year was "Solve the mystery." I would always tell our players that championships are mysteries, and they're based on unselfishness. How do you put something ahead of yourself? If you want to be a great father, put your children ahead of yourself. How do you be a great husband? Put your wife ahead of yourself. If you want to be a great teammate, put your teammates ahead of yourself. When a team does that, that's when you solve the mystery. That was a big saying around our program. I used it a bunch. Our players used that. And I remember seeing Cardale that morning, and I was like, "What in the world was that? How did that championship happen?" And he looked at me with a tear in his eye and said, "I finally learned how to solve the mystery. There was no way I was going to let J. T. Barrett and Braxton Miller down."

That was what our whole program was all about. When you hear guys talking about the brotherhood—to me, he epitomizes that. He didn't do that for the

NFL contract, unless it's something I don't know. He didn't do that for himself. He made a transformation unlike I've ever seen in my 38 years of coaching.

I don't think I used the phrase "solve the mystery." That doesn't sound like something I would have said. But he was basically right. I finally got my chance to play and help our team, and I didn't want to let my guys down. It was that simple.

In the euphoria of the win, and after not sleeping at all, I wasn't prepared for questions about my future in the press conference. I was asked about entering the NFL Draft, an idea that would have seemed ridiculous two months earlier. I said that I didn't think I was ready for the pros but didn't close the door to it. Honestly, I hadn't given it any thought. But I had to quickly. The deadline for declaring for the draft was two days away. We flew back to Columbus, and I immediately drove to Cleveland. I wanted to decompress and see my family, especially Chloe. I stayed at a friend's house because I didn't want to be hounded. I didn't answer or return anyone's texts or calls, because I just wanted to get some sleep and chill after the whirlwind of the last month and a half. I had barely slept in three or four days. I couldn't come down from the high I'd been on. My mind was still racing from what had just happened.

I had finally fallen asleep when I was woken up by a call from Coach Ginn. He asked me to come over because Coach Meyer was with him. He wanted to talk to me about some stuff. I was like, "Huh?" At the time, I didn't have Coach Meyer's cell number, so he was probably one of the people who called and texted, and I didn't know it. He probably thought I was intentionally ignoring him. So I went over to see Coach Ginn and Coach Meyer. At first, I talked with Coach Ginn about the CFP championship game and all that had just happened. We had a good laugh about everything. Tim Beck came to Cleveland with Coach Meyer. Coach Beck had just been hired to replace Tom Herman as the OSU quarterbacks coach. He introduced himself and started talking about the things we could do together. It was clear that he and Coach Meyer were trying to find out whether I was going to the NFL. "Guys, I didn't say I was leaving," I told them. But they assumed that because I hadn't responded to their texts and calls, that I was gone. I understand now why they were so concerned. With Braxton and J. T. still rehabbing their injuries, they were thinking about more than the next season. Spring practice was going to start in a couple months, and they were looking at the prospect of having no scholarship quarterbacks available except for Stephen Collier.

Urban Meyer:

We called NetJets and got a private plane to fly me from Columbus to Cleveland. I didn't know what he was going to do. I was so naive to that. I was thinking there was no way that he was ready for the National Football League. He played three games. Then people like Mark Pantoni, our top recruiting guy, told me that not only was he ready but that he might be a high draft pick. I was like, "No way." I called Ted Ginn and said, "Ted, what do you think about this thing?" And he said, "I don't know. I'm going to talk to him and talk to his family." I never really try to tell people what to do, but I asked him if I could be involved in the discussion, and Cardale said yes. I'm not sure how much homework he did on it.

I thought he might turn pro. I've done this long enough to know that people can get in your ear. There was never an indication from Ted or Cardale that he was going to leave, but I've also done this a long time.

I told them that I wasn't looking for any guarantees. Clearly, after the last three games, I felt I could be the guy. But I wasn't stupid. I knew that Braxton was really Coach Meyer's guy, and if Braxton couldn't play, J. T. was his guy. All I wanted was assurance that I would have a fair chance to win the job. Coach Meyer did not promise me anything. He didn't say that if I came back, I'd be the guy. He said that Braxton might have limitations because of his surgery and spoke briefly about possibly having different roles for him. Coach Meyer said that if I came back and took all the reps in spring practice in Braxton and J. T.'s absence, I'd put myself in a good position to be the starter. Cool. That's all I needed to hear. I told him I'd come back. My decision wasn't based only on football; I wanted to get my degree and was on track to do that. I also was a new father. The idea of entering the draft and having no control over where I lived while I had a newborn in Cleveland was unappealing. After I said I'd come back, Coach Ginn and Coach Meyer said that we had to make an announcement saying so. A press conference? I was totally opposed to that. I didn't see the need to have one. Besides, all I wanted to do was spend time with Chloe and continue to relax. But I relented and agreed to make a public announcement at Ginn Academy in a couple hours. While reporters scrambled to get to Cleveland, speculation grew that I'd be leaving. Why else would I have a press conference if not to announce I was headed to the NFL? I could kind of sense the surprise when I declared I'd be back at Ohio State for the 2015 season.

Ted Ginn Sr.:

Urban was getting ready to get on a plane to New York to do the Late Show with David Letterman. *But with Cardale having to make a decision, I told him he had to come here and talk to Cardale first. He*

> *said, "I'll see you in 45 minutes." He got here, and I found Cardale and got him in our office. Cardale felt he wasn't ready for the NFL, and that's how he made that decision.*
>
> *The press conference was not my idea. I didn't want none of that. People and the media were following Tress and trying to follow Cardale to find out the answer. People on the school board. TV stations. ESPN. People on the school board and the district were calling me. That's when Leonard "Big Jack" Jackson, head of athletics for the Cleveland Municipal School District, called me and asked me to have the press conference. There were people everywhere. Wherever Cardale went, they knew. They knew Urban was there. It was crazy.*

Who knows where I would have gone in the draft? I had those three postseason games, but that was it. Clearly, the No. 1 question was: "Where has this kid been all year?" I got wind of this about a week later, and I don't want to name any coaches, but the rumors I heard from NFL scouts were that some staff people talked about my maturity level and things they supposedly had to do to get me ready for the games. My sense was that they were trying to hurt my draft grade if I had chosen to get one as a way of influencing me to come back if I had been leaning toward leaving. I don't know if that had something to do with me not returning calls or texts after the game (because I'd blocked almost everyone). Some of the things I heard were said about me were 100 percent false.

As I said, I learned of all this after the fact. At the time, I simply didn't have time to go through all the pros and cons that I would have liked to. Players can ask the NFL for a report that gives a general conclusion about when they'll get drafted. The end of our season was such a whirlwind that I didn't even submit a report. Now I was on a tight deadline. The championship game was Monday night. We flew back Tuesday. The deadline was Thursday. I was functioning on almost zero sleep. To make a life-altering decision such as declaring for the NFL Draft when I hadn't really given it enough thought would have been a mistake, I believed. Who knows how my life and NFL career would have gone if circumstances had been different?

I have no idea where I would have gone in the 2015 draft. If you look at that draft, I probably would have been the third quarterback taken. Jameis Winston went No. 1 overall to Tampa Bay, followed immediately by Marcus Mariota to Tennessee. The third quarterback taken was Colorado State's Garrett Grayson in the third round with the 75th overall pick. Oregon's Sean Mannion went later in the third round.

The only thing I lacked was the playing experience. My three-game postseason stretch was the only meaningful playing time I had. But I didn't lack confidence in myself. I knew I had the ability. But I don't think any NFL team would have drafted me to come in and be their franchise quarterback right away based on three games. I'd be more of a developmental prospect. I would eventually question my decision to return to Ohio State, but hindsight is 20/20, right?

But I'd committed to coming back in 2015. It would be a very different year than 2014.

Chapter 18

STARTING QUARTERBACK*

After the championship, I could no longer walk on OSU's campus anonymously. I wouldn't say I enjoyed it, but I understood it. A couple of months earlier, I probably could have walked down High Street naked. Now I couldn't go anywhere without being stopped. I used to be able to run to Chipotle, grab a meal, and get to where I needed to be. I've never been someone to turn down anyone's request for a picture or quick conversation, but sometimes I was in a hurry. I wish DoorDash had been around then.

That spring was the first time we practiced in the mornings instead of the afternoons. After practice, I'd shower and go to my classes. I would often flirt with being late anyway after leaving the Woody and trying to find a parking space. My first class was American Sign Language. I always entered from the back of the room and sat in the last row as a way of not drawing attention to myself, but it came anyway. Students who weren't even in the class would knock on the door, trying to get my attention. A few times, they even busted into the class to get a picture with me. Halfway through the semester, the professor emailed coaches saying I was a distraction.

I was like, *Are you fucking kidding me?* I'll admit I was legitimately tardy for class maybe three times, but I took the class seriously. It wasn't my fault that other people sought my attention. It bothered me that the teacher didn't look at it from my perspective. She never asked if I was OK or if there was anything that could be done to accommodate me to make sure I could learn without distraction like any other student. I sent her an email saying this. I felt she was trying to establish her authority when I hadn't even tried to test it.

My social life changed too. Jeaney and I had decided not to try to get back together again and have our relationship strictly be as co-parents. She was in Cleveland with Chloe. With me being a so-called big man on campus, a long-distance romantic relationship wasn't going to work as I tried to balance helping Chloe, football, and classes. I started dating other women. I was way more cautious about whom I got involved with. I don't want to say that I didn't trust anyone, but I had to try to figure out motives. That was extremely hard. You want to be with someone who wants you for who you are, not what you might be able to provide for them or the status that being with you might carry. I just never knew. I tried to give people the benefit of the doubt while also trying to protect myself, so it was hard for me to be all in and not be guarded with whomever I was seeing at the time. I'll admit that was unfair to them.

We should have repeated as national champions in 2015. We had so much talent. Yes, we lost some key players from our title team. Devin Smith became a second-round draft pick by the New York Jets. Tight end Jeff Heuerman, who'd fought through a foot injury to be an important player for us, went to Denver in the third round. Cornerback Doran Grant was a fourth-round pick by Pittsburgh.

Jacksonville took defensive tackle Michael Bennett in the sixth round. Evan Spencer went to Washington, also in the sixth round. We also lost linebacker Curtis Grant, a leader on the 2014 defense.

But look who we had coming back: Ezekiel Elliott, Joey Bosa, Eli Apple, Taylor Decker, Pat Elflein, Billy Price, Curtis Samuel, Raekwon McMillan, Darron Lee, Mike Thomas, Jalin Marshall, Vonn Bell, Nick Vannett, Tyvis Powell, defensive tackle Adolphus Washington, and linebacker Joshua Perry. Plus several younger players with a ton of potential, such as receiver Dontre Wilson, cornerbacks Marshon Lattimore and Gareon Conley, safety Malik Hooker, and defensive ends Tyquan Lewis, Jalyn Holmes, and Sam Hubbard.

And of course, Braxton, J. T., and me at quarterback.

I'm pretty sure no college team had a quarterback room that had three players with the résumés we had. Braxton was a two-time Big Ten MVP and had finished fifth in the Heisman Trophy voting in 2012. J. T. had finished fifth in the Heisman voting in 2014. My three games as a starter to finish the previous season went okay, most people would agree.

We knew Braxton's rehab had a long way to go, but we all thought he'd be ready for the start of the 2015 season. Quarterbacks such as Drew Brees had healed fully from a torn labrum. Baseball pitchers had as well. J. T.'s broken ankle also needed a lot of time to heal, but we had no doubt he'd be ready for the season. In the pecking order, I considered myself third unless I truly played to my full potential. Braxton had two great seasons under his belt. His running ability in our spread offense gave a dimension that neither J. T. nor I—nor almost anyone on the planet—could provide. I thought it would take a lot for coaches not to go with him if he were healthy. If he weren't, I figured J. T. was next in line. He was the first OSU quarterback Coach Meyer signed, and obviously he'd gotten the starting job over me after Braxton's injury in 2014.

Still, I thought I had a great chance to be the starter. With Braxton and J. T. out for the spring, I had a chance to stake my claim. My mindset was similar to what it was in 2014 when I was battling J. T. for what we thought would be the backup job. I was going to do everything I could to give myself the best chance. I was getting all these reps they weren't. I was getting timing down with receivers that they weren't.

In spring practice, I thought I played well. It helps getting all the starter's reps. No offense to Stephen Collier, but I didn't feel I was pushed by him. I knew the real battle would be in training camp when J. T. and Braxton were back healthy. Selfishly, I wanted to show everybody that I was the guy and what we could do with me at quarterback. But I also knew what J. T. brought to the team, including his leadership. Even though he wasn't getting snaps, he still got a lot of mental reps. My goal was to put enough good plays on tape to make the decision hard for our coaches when the time came to pick a starter.

Times were different in 2015. There was no instant-transfer portal like there is now. Once I made the decision not to go to the NFL, I'd have looked like a dumbass to transfer to another school. I'd have to wait a year to play again based on the rules in effect then. Before I got my chance in 2014, I definitely was planning to transfer. After what happened when I did play, no way.

Meanwhile, my relationship with Tim Beck was developing well. I was a big fan of him and the offense he had run at Nebraska. I saw the success he'd had with Taylor Martinez when he was the Cornhuskers' quarterback. Martinez was known more for his running, but he put up some crazy numbers in the passing game as well with receivers not nearly as talented as ours. Some of the stuff in the Nebraska quarterback run game we'd already taken for our playbook. As a play caller, Beck liked a fast tempo and was aggressive, which

I liked, though we knew that our line coach, Ed Warinner, was the one promoted to take over the play-calling duties.

After spring practice, we had one last event to celebrate our national championship—our trip to the White House to see President Obama. I'm not really a political person and was even less so then. I don't know if his policies were good or bad for the country. But I know what he represented to millions of people of color like me. I remember in school on career day when we would talk about what we could be. "You can be president," we'd be told. "You can be a doctor. You can be a firefighter." But the generic faces in all those career books were all white. Not just the presidents but also the doctors and firefighters. I was like, Hold on. *My uncle is a firefighter, and he's Black. Why aren't there any pictures that look like him?* Now I know that if kids now still have those kinds of books, there's someone who looks like me.

When Obama was elected, Michelle and I were in the living room, and she cried. Not surprising for Crybaby. Now I was in Washington to meet him. First, we went to the Martin Luther King Jr. Memorial and saw the statue of him, which had just been dedicated a few years earlier. Then we went to the White House. I kept saying to somebody who worked at the White House, "Take me to the aliens. Show me where the aliens are." I was joking that there had to be something at the White House I'd never seen. "Take me to the war room. I want to press the button, bruh. We just won the championship. Make me feel special."

I think we spent more time going through security than we did with Obama, but it was pretty cool. I was standing by the door that he happened to enter through. He was like, "Cardale, how's Chloe?" and said a few things about being a dad with girls. I was like, *This motherfucker knows my kid's name.* I'm pretty sure someone gave him tips about what to say, but still, that and shaking his hand were pretty cool. I think that was the cap to the whole season.

As the spring turned to summer, it became clearer that Braxton probably wasn't going to play quarterback again. He started working out with the receivers and doing some stuff out of the backfield. During his rehab process, I'd seen him make some throws but not on real drop-backs. At some point, he made it clear he didn't want to play quarterback anymore. He said he couldn't do some of the things he used to be able to and didn't feel comfortable throwing. Becoming a wide receiver, he decided, was the next-best thing. From the outside looking in, I think he handled it really well. But there were times when he would jog off the field when receivers rotated that I could tell he missed not getting every rep as a quarterback. Every now and then, we'd put in plays with Braxton lined up at quarterback on triple-option plays. I tell you right now, if I was on defense and saw Braxton at quarterback and a backfield of Ezekiel Elliott and Curtis Samuel, I'd shit myself.

> *Urban Meyer:*
>
> *I remember Braxton coming to me and saying, "I think I should learn the receiver position." I was very close to Braxton, and we had long talks. I think he kind of accepted the fact that it was time to move on, and his best chance of making the National Football League was by playing another position.*

We went into camp that summer with so much firepower on offense that we didn't know just how good we could be. Then we had our first scrimmage. We looked horrible. It didn't get much better as camp progressed. J. T. and I split the reps, with me getting maybe slightly more. It was clearly the most intense camp battle I'd been in, with so much at stake. With the sprinkling in of Braxton quarterback plays and coaches trying to incorporate some of the things I did well and some of the things J. T. did well, it was just a clusterfuck. We couldn't establish any real rhythm during camp.

Our play-calling was completely different. We tried to get too cute with all the offensive talent we had. Instead of just running our offense and exploiting what we saw from opposing defenses, coaches decided to design plays to get certain guys touches. They were trying to keep guys happy, even though that wasn't an issue. No one was selfish. No one was demanding touches. We just wanted to win and play well. We knew if we did, the stats would come and we'd all be content.

We were ranked No. 1 when the season started. Our opener was in Blacksburg, Virginia, against Virginia Tech, the team that had exposed our flaws and youth the year before in Columbus. All summer, the burning question in college football was about who would start for us at quarterback. We had no idea. The week of the game, J. T. and I were still splitting reps. Our game plan that week included a lot of quarterback runs. That was more J. T.'s strength than mine, so I thought there was no way I would start. But only Coach Meyer knew. The day before the game, I asked Coach Beck who was starting. He said he didn't know but that he thought both of us would play. That wasn't what either of us wanted. Our styles were so different. We'd struggled in camp when we were sharing reps largely because of that.

J. T. Barrett:

Coach Meyer never said who was starting that game. Would I have preferred to know? Absolutely!

Urban Meyer:

I had the mindset—and always have—that if you're the starting quarterback, which at that point Cardale was, you've got to beat him out.... Whoever's the No. 1 quarterback, you've got to beat him out. That's the approach I took. Cardale was the starting quarterback at the end of the year, and J. T. had to beat him out. In my mind, Cardale would have to lose his spot to J. T. And we never felt that happened during training camp.

You had one guy who made a historic run that will never be matched again in Cardale. You had another guy who was arguably one of the greatest leaders I'd ever been around and took us right up to winning a championship in a phenomenal freshman year and would later break Drew Brees's records. We had a dilemma. But in my mind, Cardale earned the right to start. I also factored in that J. T. was going to have another year after 2015 and this was likely to be Cardale's final year at Ohio State.

During pregame warm-ups, we both took reps with the ones. During Virginia Tech's opening drive, we still didn't know. J. T. and I were giving each other awkward looks. When we got the ball, Coach Meyer looked at me and said, "Cardale, go." That was it. I didn't have time to have what that meant sink in. The play clock was already running and we had to get lined up and going. The first play was a quarterback run. I would run 13 times that night for 99 yards. We jumped to a quick 14–0 lead. I threw to Curtis Samuel, who caught a 24-yard pass despite being interfered with, for our first touchdown. On our next series, Zeke ran 80 yards for our second score.

Virginia Tech rallied in the second quarter and took a 17–14 lead into halftime. The second half became Braxton's wide receiver coming-out party. After I ran for 20 yards to our 46-yard line, I threw to Braxton, who'd gotten behind his guy. He made the catch and shook off a tackle for a 54-yard score to give us the lead. That was just a warm-up for his second score. He took the handoff, turned left and found some running room. Virginia Tech had two tacklers who had the angle on Braxton. But he left them in the dust with a spin move that looked like it came out of a video game and ran for a 53-yard touchdown to make it 28–17. In between Braxton's touchdowns, Virginia Tech quarterback Billy Brewer was knocked out of the game with a broken collarbone when Adolphus Washington hit him as he threw. I threw to Johnnie Dixon for a 29-yard gain and then ran in from 10 yards to make it 35–17. J. T. then came in and led us on a 75-yard drive that ended with a 26-yard touchdown pass to Mike Thomas. Virginia Tech scored a meaningless touchdown late to make the final score 42–24.

I had completed 10 of 19 passes for 187 yards and thrown one interception. All in all, I thought I played okay and had done enough to solidify my status as a starter. I thought I did well with the mental part of the game. The coaches had a great game plan, and I thought I made good checks against Virginia Tech defensive coordinator Bud Foster's scheme. I just remember being sore from the pounding I'd taken running the ball so much.

Our fans had that Virginia Tech game circled, for obvious reasons. We passed that test, winning against a good team on the road in prime time with all the pressure on us. We'd be huge favorites against our next three nonconference opponents: Hawaii, Northern Illinois, and Western Michigan. Nobody expected them to give us trouble. But those games were a sign of the struggles we'd have in 2015.

We were more than 40-point favorites over Hawaii but led only 17–0 at halftime before pulling away for a 38–0 win. I didn't play well, throwing for only 111 yards and no touchdowns, and I fumbled twice, though we recovered both. By no means was it an impressive performance—by me or the team. But it was a win, and a lopsided one, and that's hard to do in college football, especially when everybody is shooting for you like they were in 2015.

J. T. Barrett:

Regardless of who was quarterback, it was frustrating to see the trouble we had moving the ball. We looked like we didn't know what we were doing. We won 38–0 against the University of Hawaii, and I can tell you after that game, it felt like we'd lost.

The media talked it up too. I don't know if people recognize that Coach Meyer read all of that. Like when they said the deep passing game was struggling, that was a conversation every single day. I only say that because it impacted our offense. That's all I'd hear about, how I couldn't throw a deep ball, like the year before we didn't throw a deep pass. More than anything, it was because we didn't call deep-pass plays.

It was after that game that I sensed that Coach Meyer preferred J. T. as his starter. I still didn't have much of a relationship with Coach Meyer, nothing like I imagined you'd see between a head coach and a quarterback. I was dealing almost totally with Coach Beck. I felt Coach Meyer was starting to blame me for the offense underachieving. The next week was an ugly 20–13 win over Northern Illinois. I threw two interceptions and got benched. J. T. came in and wasn't much better, also throwing a pick. We needed a pick-six by Darron Lee to stretch our lead to 20–10 or things might have been truly scary. The next week was somewhat better. We beat Western Michigan 38–12. I threw for 288 yards but also had an interception and was off on some deep throws.

Overall, we were just out of sync as we headed into conference play. The year before, we knew who was in charge of the offense—Tom Herman. In 2015 it was a hodgepodge, and it showed, especially in the red zone, where we really struggled.

> *J. T. Barrett:*
>
> *There was a lot behind the scenes that was shaking. Coach Meyer didn't trust the person calling the plays. First or second down, Coach Warinner might call the play. Coach Meyer might call the play if it was a shot play, or if it was a pass play, Coach Beck might make the call. If it was a third down, Coach [Zach] Smith [wide receivers coach] would call the play.*
>
> *What? I didn't know what was coming out as the quarterback. Whereas the year before, I knew exactly what was happening. I knew where Coach Herman wanted the ball. I knew where the ball was supposed to go. I knew which plays I liked and which plays I didn't like. We had answers for different coverages. It wasn't, "Hey, get this guy the ball." All those things played a part.*

Both J. T. and I were playing really badly. We had conversations all the time about it, like, "This is terrible." J. T. and I would get on the phone with Tom Herman every other week. Herman called us and said, "Man, you guys stink."

Urban Meyer:

We lost Tom Herman, who was obviously a phenomenal coach, and we were in a little bit of disarray on offense. We just couldn't really perform at the level we hoped.

We struggled the next week at Indiana, a team we hadn't lost to since 1988. We fell behind 10–0 before rallying to win 34–27 after an Indiana pass from our 9-yard line fell incomplete on the last play of the game. I completed 18 of 27 passes for 245 yards with a touchdown and an interception. But once again we struggled in the red zone. The next week against Maryland, Coach Meyer decided to make J. T. the designated red zone quarterback.

It worked against the Terrapins. I threw two touchdown passes on 21-of-28 passing for 291 yards. J. T. ran for three as we pulled away for a 49–28 win. Our play-calling was smooth because Coach Beck took over those duties for that game. But a two-quarterback system almost never works for long. What's the saying, "When you have two quarterbacks, you really have none"? I know that Coach Meyer used it at Florida when Chris Leak was a senior and Tim Tebow was a freshman. Leak played most of the snaps with Tebow in for short-yardage runs or at the goal line.

But this was different. We were both veteran quarterbacks who'd led the team to success in a full-time role. It was hard for me to be the quarterback knowing that if we got close to scoring, I'd be replaced. Don't put me in a situation when I feel I've got to make something happen in three snaps because if we pass the opposing 40-yard line, I'll get replaced. Don't put me in that mindset. And don't put our team in that, because you change the whole dynamic of play-calling. You change the entire rhythm when you do things like that. It also affects leadership. Your guys need to know who they're looking to and who's going to hold each other accountable. I'm not saying you can't have two leaders. But to have two quarterbacks in that position? Come on, man. You're screwing everybody. You're also putting yourself in a situation where now your receivers have their favorite quarterback. They're thinking, *OK, I know when he's in, I'm getting the ball, and if the other is in, I'm just going through the motions.*

I finally did have a meeting with Coach Meyer and talked about this stuff. He tried to question my competitiveness by asking if I had aspirations of playing at the next level. Of course I did. "You think those guys don't look over their shoulder?" he said. I said that I was sure that when those guys were walking off the field after a three-and-out on the first possession, they didn't see their backup warming up. In 2014 I'd accepted my backup role when J. T. began playing really well, and Tom Herman explained to me that he didn't want to have a quarterback battle during the season. Right after we won the championship and I had to decide about the NFL, I did not ask Coach Meyer to promise me the starting job. I just wanted a legitimate chance to compete. Now he was using my competitiveness against me because I wanted clarity in my role. That's when I started to lose confidence in my role on the team and faith in the coaching staff.

Coach Meyer and I were night and day in terms of background and personality. He commands a room, in my opinion, with fear and authority. I command it by making people comfortable and often with laughter. I think that's effective, because when I do have to say something serious, it hits home a little differently because I'm normally lighthearted. I'm not going to be a guy who's MFing you 24/7. I understand that mistakes are going to happen, and we've got to bounce back from them. I always approach it the way I would like someone to approach it with me if I was down in the dumps because I threw a bad pass or an interception. Don't get me wrong: There's a time and place to put your foot down. But I don't think it's every time and in every situation. After we won the championship in 2014, Coach Meyer made a comment that "Your guys just go for you," and told me not to change. But when I was younger, he just said, "You've gotta change. You've gotta change."

I just didn't really have a relationship with Coach Meyer. He didn't recruit me. He *inherited* me. If he had been the coach at Ohio State during my recruitment and gotten to know me, I don't think he would have offered me a scholarship. I don't think it would have mattered if I were a 30-star player. I just don't think I fit the characteristics of what he was looking for in a quarterback. There were times he would say to me, "Why can't you be more like Tim Tebow or Alex Smith, who was a No. 1 overall pick?" He was referring to the way I carried myself, not my performance or ability. I think that's what drove him crazy. Before I became the starter at the end of 2014, it was only rarely that I did something positive to open his eyes about me or even pay me much attention. But then I'd be late to class or a tutoring session. Coach Meyer wanted a quarterback who had the whole package, especially as a leader and face of the team. In his eyes, I didn't have it all, on or off the field.

I once made a comment that Coach Meyer ruined my experience at Ohio State. That's at least misleading. I committed to Ohio State because of Coach Tressel. Coach Tressel and his staff were more nurturing. He had more of a family environment, like, "Let me help you be the best player and person you can be here." Coach Meyer was, "How can you help the team?" I think it was such a shock going into that environment *expecting* it to be the way Coach Tressel ran the program and experiencing the way Coach Meyer did.

Urban Meyer:

I think I'm Joe Serious, and he wants a smile on his face. Yeah, we're pretty different. But I think we're also probably a little more similar than we think too, like when I said that the reason he changed was that he never wanted to let Braxton and J. T. down. I think I'm a lot like that. I don't ever really do anything for myself. Why do I get so uptight about coaching? Because I don't want to let players down.

By the time we played Penn State, I could kind of see the writing on the wall. In our game plan, we called for things that were more J. T.'s forte than mine. Penn State always played us tough, and they did in 2015 as well. We got only one first down in our first three possessions. When we finally got a drive going, J. T. replaced me in the red zone and ran for a five-yard touchdown. Our next possession, J. T. took over when we were at the Penn State 31 and finished that touchdown drive. At halftime, I changed my Twitter bio to "Backup quarterback at Ohio State." I got two more series in the third quarter before J. T. replaced me for good in our 38–10 win. He threw only four times, completing all of them, but ran for more than 100 yards.

The next morning, Coach Beck texted me and asked me to get to the Woody a little early. I knew what was coming. We went into Coach Meyer's office, and he said, "We're going to go with J. T. this week." I said, "I'm not stupid. I know you guys wanted J. T. the whole time. I'm good. I know my role now."

Our offense under J. T. looked completely different the next week. We had 528 yards of offense in a 49–7 win over Rutgers. J. T. was 14-of-18 for 223 yards and three touchdowns and ran for 101 yards and two scores.

> *Tyvis Powell:*
>
> *To be honest, Cardale never really truly felt like he was a starter. He just felt he was kind of a replacement until he messed up and J. T. could go in. I think that messed with him mentally because he felt he had no job security. That's part of life, but to be successful in college football, I think you have to have your coaches behind you. I think the offense struggled because Herman left. That was a huge hit to our offense because he was an offensive genius, in my opinion. The new guys coming in just could not figure out how to call plays.*
>
> *Another issue was that certain people were promised a certain number of targets. I think that played a part in the play-calling, and it made everything just look bad. But I will say that when J. T. got into a game, for some odd reason our offense produced a tad bit more. I don't know what that was about. I want to say it's because he was more mobile. Maybe that was why. But for some reason, when J. T. went in, the offense started rolling. I know the receivers took a vote on who they wanted at quarterback. I think the majority of them, if not all of them, except for one—Corey Smith—said they wanted J. T. at quarterback.*

After Rutgers and heading into the game two weeks later against Minnesota after an off week, I had no expectations of playing. Then the Saturday night after we were off, I got a call from J. T. He had driven up to a police checkpoint on campus. There was a long line of traffic, and J. T. thought it was construction and tried to back up and avoid it. Police stopped him and gave him a Breathalyzer, and he flunked the test. I had friends in town and was actually out with them. J. T. was with a girl, and she had been drinking too. So J. T. called me and I drove 10 or 15 minutes to pick him up. When I got there, the police officer said he had passed the walking test and wasn't swerving, but he had blown over the limit. The policeman said there was no need to arrest J. T. but that the report of his OVI (operating a vehicle impaired) would come out the next morning. I was like, *Shit*. I took J. T. and the girl home. I'm sure he felt his life was flashing before his eyes.

> *J. T. Barrett:*
>
> *He was there for me, so I really appreciated it. I thought it was going to be the end of the world. He was saying, "It's going to be OK. Keep your head up." Drinking before driving was just poor judgment by me. I didn't know what a checkpoint was. Where I'm from, I'd never seen one. I thought it was traffic.*
>
> *I learned a lot from that. I don't drink and drive to this day because of that. Some things you go through, at the time you think it's the worst thing ever. But you can learn and grow from it.*

J. T. got suspended for the Minnesota game, so I played the next week against the Golden Gophers, a team that always played us tough. We beat them 28–14 in a sloppy performance. I completed 12 of 22 passes for 187 yards and a touchdown pass to Mike Thomas. I had a 38-yard touchdown run to ice the game with just fewer than two minutes left. My assessment after the game about our offense was that we played below average. Still, I thought I'd done enough to earn another start. I was wrong. I didn't know it at the time, but I'd never take another snap in a Buckeyes uniform. I can't say I was shocked that J. T. was reinserted the next week against Illinois. I was cool with it. I accepted my backup role again. Besides, by that point, I knew what the staff was thinking and had kind of lost respect for those guys, honestly. We beat Illinois 28–3 to set up what would become the defining game of the 2015 season.

Chapter 19

A DISAPPOINTING END

OUR MAIN RIVAL was the Team Up North. Nothing would ever change that. But during my Ohio State career, our toughest Big Ten test usually came against Michigan State, coached by former OSU assistant coach Mark Dantonio. We beat the Spartans 17–16 in East Lansing in 2012 in a game that was the turning point in our undefeated season. They beat us in the Big Ten Football Championship Game in 2013, denying us a chance for the national title. We hammered them in our 2014 showdown up there.

Now we'd face them in the Shoe. We'd slipped to No. 3 in the CFP rankings but were still undefeated. Michigan State was No. 9. The Spartans had won a miracle game against Michigan when the Wolverines botched a punt on the final play of the game and the Spartans scored a game-winning touchdown. Their only loss was 39–38 at Nebraska. Michigan State's star quarterback, Connor Cook, injured his shoulder the week before our game against Maryland, so the Spartans had to go with backups. We weren't at full strength either. Zeke had been in the hospital that week because of an infection in his leg.

The weather was terrible—cold, rainy, and windy. Our offensive performance was worse. We got only five first downs and gained just 132 yards, the lowest total in Coach Meyer's entire career. The only two touchdowns we scored came on short fields after Michigan State turnovers. Still, we never trailed until the final play when Michael Geiger kicked a 41-yard field goal and then windmilled his right arm in celebration—and through our hearts.

Against a team like Michigan State, which plays aggressively, you have to take deep shots. I know the weather made that harder, but we only tried it once or twice. We had no rhythm to our offense and got too cute on some of our designed runs. We got outcoached. I felt it throughout the week. I felt it throughout the season. Some of the stuff the coaches kept trying to do with some of the players—all of this cute shit, like, "It's Senior Day and let's make sure Braxton gets this many touches" instead of worrying about going out and just winning the game.

After the game, Zeke, who had only 12 carries, ripped our play-calling. He was right. He apologized to the team later, which I didn't think he should have done. Coaches bashed us when we didn't play well, but we couldn't say anything critical when they didn't coach well? I didn't understand that.

Urban Meyer:

Of course it bothered me. But I guess I have more understanding for players than most, and so I brought Zeke and his family in, and we had a good chat about it. I think it was something about how he needed to carry the ball more. I agreed with him. But the reality was that we were playing Michigan State, which was one of the top teams nationally in rush defense, and we were not able to throw the ball because of the weather. That was a bad day.

When we were struggling, I thought I was going to get an opportunity to play. I said something to Coach Beck at halftime about needing to take some shots downfield. But they stuck with J. T. He was their guy.

J. T. Barrett:

In that game, we were doing things we'd never done on offense. We were creating plays thinking they were designing their defense to stop the plays used the year before, but they didn't stop them. Ultimately it relied a lot on me running the ball. People also know the conditions in that game. It was so weird. It was like the perfect storm for them to win that game on that field with Connor Cook out.

Zeke missed all practices that week, and that required me to run the ball a lot. All the years I was asked to run the ball, I didn't ask for that. That was more so Coach Meyer doing that out of comfort because he saw Braxton do that. I didn't sign up to be a running back that played quarterback. I signed up to be a quarterback.

Tyvis Powell:

That was the first time we felt betrayed by our coaches. It's kind of like they just folded their cards. That was the huge conversation after the game with me, Zeke, Mike, and Cardale, because I remember us walking off the field and cussing the coaching staff out, like they kind of sold us up the river in that game.

In the locker room, everybody was rushing to get out of there because we didn't want to be around the coaches. We felt they had let us down. Coach Beck or Coach Warinner was talking to us as we got dressed—I can't remember which one. If I was asked to repeat one word he said for $1 million, I'd be pissed because I would lose that $1 million.

> *Urban Meyer:*
>
> *That might have been the worst loss I had at Ohio State, because I felt we could have done better as a coaching staff. You wish you had some calls over again during that game with the rainstorm. In that kind of environment, we had a really hard time.*

The next week, we put it on Michigan 42–13. Zeke ran for more than 200 yards and we dominated the second half. A victory over Michigan was always sweet, but when I didn't even get a snap in mop-up time, I was like, *Fuck these guys*, from Urban on down. I thought of Kenny Guiton and how he felt in the final games of his career in 2013 when he realized that was it and they had no plans for him and didn't believe in him enough to let him play at least a little. I had that feeling leaving the locker room in Ann Arbor.

Tim Beck called the plays in the Michigan game, and I remember texting him after the game to congratulate him on his play-calling, which was damn near flawless. I said that if we were going to have success in the future, he would have to be the play caller. We'd had conversations earlier about trying to get the coaching staff to respect his input more. It reminded me of 2012 when Tom Herman was in his first year. Even though he was the coordinator, Coach Meyer really was the coordinator. He had too much say-so, and it threw off Coach Herman's rhythm. In about the fourth or fifth game of that season, Coach Herman was doing his thing and we were on a roll. He was trying to get his play down to the play callers on the field. I was wearing a headset as a backup quarterback, and Coach Meyer said, "No, let's run this instead." And Coach Herman went, "No, I've fucking got it!" and kind of put Coach Meyer in his place, which he respected. From then on, everything went smoothly when Coach Herman was calling plays, especially when he got into a rhythm.

In 2015, with Ed Warinner as the coordinator, Coach Meyer was doing the same thing he did in early 2012, throwing his two cents in: "Call this. Do this. Now get it to Braxton." I was like, *This is horrible.* I could only imagine these guys on the headset trying to get the signal in.

If Penn State had upset Michigan State in their regular-season finale, we would have gotten another chance to play in the CFP. But the Spartans took care of business. They then beat undefeated Iowa in the Big Ten championship before eventual national champion Alabama smoked them 38–0 in the CFP semifinals. Bama was fortunate it didn't have to play us. We would have destroyed the Crimson Tide. I don't care how bad the coaches were coaching that game or that year, if we'd gotten a chance to play them, we'd have kicked their ass.

Instead of having a chance to repeat, we finished our season in the Fiesta Bowl against Notre Dame. We won 44–28, with the offense clicking again with Tim Beck calling the plays. We finished 12–1, but it was not the season we wanted or expected to have. We had so much talent, so many guys who'd go on to play in the NFL. But it just never really clicked the way it should have until the last two games.

Urban Meyer:

It wasn't easy. I'd been through that before at Florida—when you're preseason No. 1 coming off a

> *championship, and it's just not easy to coach. There were a lot of personalities on that team. There were a lot of guys thinking about the NFL. We'd lost coaches, and so it didn't go as well as we'd hoped. But for someone to say we mismanaged something, I'd probably say, "What the hell are you talking about?" We went 12–1. We lost a game in a rainstorm. If I would have started J. T. over Cardale to start the season, that would have been a story. When we made the quarterback change, it was because we weren't doing well on offense, whether that was a new quarterback coach or the chemistry, which I kind of heard things about later on. But that's what happens on teams sometimes.*

I didn't play in the Fiesta Bowl, even with the outcome settled. I had a mixture of feelings. I was happy for our team to win, but I was down because I didn't play. My mindset was more like, *On to bigger and better things.* I know college football is a business, but I'd be headed to the NFL, where it would be nothing but business; you couldn't get personal feelings involved. It wouldn't be about the Block O. It wouldn't be about the brotherhood. There would be none of that in the NFL. It would be all about what you could do for the team.

As I took off my Ohio State uniform for the last time after the Fiesta Bowl, I questioned my decision to return for the 2015 season instead of leaving riding high off a national championship. *I came back for this?* With the ups and downs that we had that year, particularly me, I missed out on a chance to be in the NFL, maybe to have been a high draft pick, which would have set me up better financially. I missed out on a lot, for almost a lie. Coach Meyer didn't promise me anything when I said I'd come back in 2015. But I didn't even come close to meeting the expectations I had for that year. Was the journey I went through in 2015 really worth it?

As I sat in the locker room as a Buckeyes player for the last time, all the emotions hit me. And I bawled my eyes out.

Chapter 20

ENTERING THE NFL

I DIDN'T HAVE MUCH TIME to dwell on the end of my Ohio State career. It was time to prepare for the NFL Draft. Honestly, after the shitty year I had in 2015, I wondered if my draft stock had sunk so much that I wouldn't even be taken. Back then, the NCAA had not allowed immediate transfers. If that had been an option, I would have considered it. No way would I have gone back to Ohio State. I'd have wanted a fresh start.

But under the old transfer rules, I would have had to sit out a year. I wasn't willing to do that. I would have had to learn a new playbook and scheme quickly, adapt to new coaches and teammates. Then there was the academic side. I would have had to take a heavier course load than I was willing to if I'd changed schools. It wasn't really something I considered seriously.

So it was on to the NFL Draft for me. It's a super weird process going from the college football season to Combine training and through the draft process. It feels like the longest year of your life as a player. After we returned from Arizona, I was in Columbus for only about three or four days before flying to San Diego to start getting ready for the NFL Combine a couple months later. I trained with Jamal Liggin to improve my speed, strength, and agility. I worked with quarterbacks coach George Whitfield Jr. for more position-specific drills.

I flew to Indianapolis for the Combine. The first I did were medical exams. For some players, the medicals are a big deal. I was fortunate. My medicals were clean. The only thing I'd ever had at Ohio State was a minor arthroscopic procedure to clean up cartilage my freshman year. I was able to run full speed four days afterward. I honestly cannot remember which knee it was on. The ports they used for the incisions didn't leave scars. I'd also jammed my pinkie finger taking a snap in practice at the Fiesta Bowl and had to have that X-rayed. That's it.

The medical exams were done in a bunch of ballrooms at the hotel. I sat at a table in compression shorts as team doctors examined me. They were bending me and twisting my limbs and neck. I went to the next room, and I went through the same thing. And the next. I wanted to tell the doctors that I'd just had the same exam by every other doctor there, but I understood why each team wanted their doctors to examine me. If they drafted a player, they'd invested in him and his body, and they needed to know if there was something that would prevent them from getting a return on that investment.

I got a little rest after the medical exam, but then I met with representatives from NFL teams. Sometimes it was the whole staff, and other times it was just some staffers or even just the coach. When I met with the Steelers, the first thing Coach Mike Tomlin said was, "Man, I hate your social media. I hate your Twitter game." He asked how I would manage social media in the pros and whether it would be a distraction. Some coaches just wanted to talk ball or get to know me better. Some wanted to get under my skin to see how I'd react. When I met with one team—I think it was the Eagles, but I'm not sure—there was a scout in the back of the room who was just an asshole. He asked me to describe a typical day in detail. It seemed like he wanted a complete description. So I gave him one, more than he possibly could have wanted.

The on-field drills were the last thing I did. Unfortunately, I tweaked my hamstring during my second 40-yard dash and couldn't do anything else. What would normally be a two-and-a-half-hour drive back to Columbus took me about six hours because I kept getting spasms in my hamstrings and had to pull over repeatedly. It felt like I'd gotten shot. Other than the ankle I sprained before the 2014 Michigan State game, it was the most painful injury I've had.

Ohio State had its Pro Day at the Woody Hayes Athletic Center a few weeks later, and I did fine. It was the last time my Ohio State teammates would be together, and it was cool to see everybody again after we'd been scattered around the country training. We knew how much work each of us had put in to get to that point, so we were excited not just personally but for each other. But we were all so busy with meetings that we didn't really get a chance to say goodbye to each other as a group. It felt more like a "Good luck" than a "Goodbye."

I flew down to do Jon Gruden's *QB Camp* show, which was cool. I was a Gruden fan. He was super innovative when it came to offense and used complex verbiage, so I looked forward to that challenge. We did some stuff on the whiteboard and then did some on-field drills. Bruce Irvin, who had just signed a big contract with the Raiders, rushed off the edge to simulate what I'd see in an NFL game. Former Buckeyes receiver Santonio Holmes was one of my receivers. I was like, *This is amazing.* I also flew to Los Angeles for some media stuff with the NFL Network and ESPN. I also did private workouts with teams. One I did for the Chargers would occur in Cleveland. I recruited Shane Winn and another high school teammate who wasn't even playing anymore, Nicholas Davis, to run routes for me.

Not long before the draft, Coach Meyer was asked about my NFL potential. He said a lot of complimentary things about my ability, intelligence, and growth but added that the team that drafted me would have to be patient to develop me. He was also quoted as saying that I "wasn't necessarily very good at school." His comments became a national story. I happened to see it on ESPN when Stephen A. Smith ripped him for saying that. I turned on the TV in the middle of the segment and didn't realize right away that it was about me. Before that, I had been ready to mostly bury the hatchet with Coach Meyer. Now I was like, *Fuck that.* It felt like he was trying to sabotage me. Coach Meyer texted me with a long message explaining that his comments were taken out of context. I didn't respond.

Urban Meyer:

As a coach, you get asked a lot of questions about your players. I was always very positive about Cardale. But when NFL people did their research on his academic background, I'm sure they asked about it. I got asked a little bit about school, and I said that yeah, he struggled a little bit in school. But in my recollection, I was extremely complimentary of what Cardale did and his growth and maturity because it was something I'd never experienced in my coaching career. He really grew up.

Finally, the draft arrived. I had no clue when I'd get picked. My agents at the time said the third round would be the earliest I'd go, but the fourth round was more realistic. I watched the first round because I knew a lot of my teammates would go then. Five did: Joey Bosa, Ezekiel Elliott, Eli Apple, Taylor Decker, and Darron Lee—all in the first 20 picks. But I didn't even watch the draft the next two days. I didn't want a draft party, which kind of pissed off my family. But I told them that it wasn't a big deal to me. I still had to make a team. I told them we could celebrate some other time when I'd done something to merit it.

Even on the last day of the draft, I wasn't watching it. I had a couple buddies and my brother Jay at my apartment in Columbus who were watching. I was taking a nap in my bedroom when I got a call from the Buffalo Bills saying they were taking me in the fourth round. In hindsight, it was clear Buffalo was interested in me. I came out and told everyone there. During my OSU pro day, Bills quarterbacks coach David Lee had coached me up afterward because I'd thrown a few passes behind receivers on drag routes. He was also interested in meeting my mom. The Bills were one of the teams that brought me in for a visit before the draft.

After I took the phone call from the Bills, Jay had some champagne and sprayed me. That stuff stings. I was like, "I can't see," and walked right into a wall. When they flashed my name on the screen, that was a pretty sweet moment. But that wore off pretty fast. I just wanted to know how quickly I needed to get to Buffalo.

Chapter 21

THINGS DON'T ALWAYS GO AS PLANNED

As my NFL career was about to begin, I knew I had one baby to support. Chloe was one year old. I then found out that I would become a father again, and not just once but twice. My son Carter was born in February. My son Owen was born in June. Yes, they were surprises. Yes, it was extremely awkward. Both were the result of relationships that broke up before I knew the moms were pregnant. As I've said, I'd never wanted to have kids by more than one woman, but life doesn't always go as planned. Some moms-to-be don't show until pretty late into pregnancy. Carter's mom, Sabrina, didn't until she was six months along. After we broke up, I started dating Owen's mom, Morgan. She also didn't realize she was pregnant for the first four months. I took the paternity tests, which proved they were mine. Obviously, the circumstances were not ideal, but there was nothing I could do about that. All I could do was love and support my babies.

When you're drafted, you have a rookie minicamp the next weekend. Fortunately, I'd have an Ohio State teammate with me. Buffalo had drafted Adolphus Washington in the third round. Adolphus, who's from Cincinnati, and I had known each other since we took our recruiting visit to Ohio State at the same time. We roomed together for the Bills' rookie minicamp before we each found our own places for the season.

As a fourth-round draft pick, I knew I wouldn't be expected to play right away. I just wanted to learn everything I could. I think the biggest eye-opener for me going to the NFL was how much more I needed to do on my own. In the NFL, there are short minicamps, but there's no extended spring practice like in college. If you don't manage your time right, you can put yourself in a bad position. You can't think that you can take a big vacation between minicamps and training camp. Especially as a rookie, you have to master the playbook as much as possible and make sure you stay in great shape.

Part of what I also learned in Buffalo was how the NFL really does stand for Not For Long. Our offensive coordinator, Greg Roman, was fired after the second game of the season. Our head coach, Rex Ryan, was fired before the last game of the year. General manager Doug Whaley would be fired the following April. That was such a toxic situation to be in during my first year, because I still didn't understand the business of pro football yet.

I was behind Tyrod Taylor and EJ Manuel on the quarterback depth chart. Taylor signed as a free agent the year before and went to the Pro Bowl in 2015. Manuel had been a first-round pick in 2013. Both were still young guys who weren't really able to take me under their wing the way a veteran could, but I did learn a lot from them. EJ had experienced his struggles—that's why they signed Tyrod—but I was impressed by how amazingly he dealt with adversity. EJ always handled his business so that he'd be ready for his next opportunity.

I learned from them and others why some have longer NFL careers than others. The ones who are successful have established a routine and hold themselves accountable to it. So many first- and second-year guys get in trouble off the field because they have plenty of money and free time for the first time and don't know how to handle it. I was careful with my money. I'd gotten a signing bonus of $388,393, and my salary was $450,000. I'd also made a decent amount of money from signing memorabilia after my OSU season ended. Other than a decked-out Jeep—I finally said goodbye to my 2006 Dalemobile—I didn't spend extravagantly. I paid off Michelle's car payment and invested probably 90 percent of the rest of my money. I don't think I even realized right away when the signing bonus money went into my bank account. But it was cool to know I had that money. It mainly made me think about all the little things I knew my family couldn't afford for me as a kid. I wondered how many Hot Wheels toy cars I could have gotten back then with that money. But I never really had a lot of wants as a kid because I knew I couldn't get them. I never became materialistic as a result. I like designer fashion, but if I could wear sweats every day, I would.

Having money was nice, but the harsh nature of the NFL hit me early. We got off to an 0–2 start. That's when they fired Roman. We had just taken our team picture earlier that day. I was just like, *This is insane.* It was tough to see the business side of things like that. We won our next four games but then lost three straight. We followed that by winning two in a row to give ourselves a shot at the playoffs, only to lose the next two games. There's no worse feeling than to play out the string knowing you're not going to the postseason. By then, the cracks on our team were out in the open. Rex Ryan and Doug Whaley didn't get along, or at least didn't share the same vision. Offensive coordinator Anthony Lynn finished the season as head coach.

In the midst of this, I finally got my chance to play. The team didn't want Tyrod to play the final game of the year because, I believe, the Bills didn't want him to reach certain contract incentives. EJ started the finale against the Jets. When he struggled, I relieved him. I did decently until I threw an interception that bounced off my receiver's hands and Darrelle Revis intercepted it. I was 6-for-11 for 96 yards, with the longest completion a 64-yarder to Justin Hunter. Coach Lynn had called for something else, but I waved him off and threw a bomb to Justin. Coach Lynn told me much later that if I hadn't completed that pass, he'd have benched my ass. We ended up losing 18–14. Little did I know that it would be the only time I'd play in a regular-season NFL game.

After my first NFL season, I had one more thing to finish at Ohio State: getting my diploma. I finished up my credits and in May 2017 I graduated with a degree in African American and African studies. I wore my graduation cap and gown. On the cap, I couldn't resist putting a reference to my famous tweet from five years earlier: "Sum 1 ONCE SAID, 'We Ain't Come Here to Play School.'" I think it was just a funny way of capping off the journey of my academic career and what people thought of me at the time of the tweet. Probably 90 percent of the comments and tweets and what the media said about me and my character was critical. But I'm pretty sure people did 10 times worse stuff than that, so it was kind of a fuck you to everybody who said something, honestly.

After graduation, it was back to Buffalo. It had become clear in the off-season that whatever NFL future I would have, it wouldn't be in Buffalo. Anthony Lynn left to become head coach of the Los Angeles Chargers. Sean McDermott was hired as the Bills' new coach in January. A day before Doug Whaley was fired, Buffalo took another quarterback, Nathan Peterman, in the draft.

Because we had a new coach, the Bills were allowed to start our off-season training program two weeks early. Even though the people in charge when I was drafted were now gone, I looked at it as a fresh start with a clean slate. EJ was gone, so Tyrod and I were the returning quarterbacks. In addition to Peterman, the team signed veteran T. J. Yates as a free agent.

Throughout the spring and summer, new general manager Brandon Beane cut a lot of the players from the old regime. I was still with the team when training camp started in Rochester, but not for long. The first day of camp, we had our conditioning test, which I passed. We had our first meetings that night, but my time with the Bills didn't even last through those meetings. That evening, I was told I'd been traded to the Chargers. The Bills got a seventh-round draft pick for me. I had no hard feelings. I'd be reunited with Anthony Lynn, whom I liked. I thanked the Bills for the opportunity, and that was it. I jumped in my car and drove an hour to my home in suburban Buffalo, packed my stuff, and drove to Cleveland.

I flew to L.A. the next morning. The Chargers were just about to start camp, which began with their conditioning test. When Coach Lynn called me right after he traded for me, I jokingly asked if I could just use the Bills' conditioning test for my Chargers one. We laughed about that and he said he'd take care of me. Coach Lynn wasn't on the field as we did our conditioning tests. Mind you, my legs were dead from the long flight across the country and my Bills conditioning test. I was like, *Jesus, this is not going to go well.* We had to do 300-yard shuttles. We started from the 50-yard line and ran to the end zone and back three times. We'd do a similar drill at Ohio State, but in Columbus we only had to average a certain time for the whole drill. In the Chargers' test, we had to hit a certain time in all three legs. Before the second leg, I thought to myself, *I'm gonna die. This is about to be the most embarrassing thing because*

I'm going to fail the test. Somehow I did pass the second leg. But I still had the final leg to run. Coach Lynn finally came out to the field and saw me. "Cardale, what are you doing? Stop." I was like, "Oh my God! Thank God!" I was not going to pass that third one, I can promise. My legs were gone.

The next day was our first real practice, and my legs still felt horrible. Sure enough, my first practice rep was a naked bootleg. I rolled out, and it felt like my legs were not moving. I kind of stumbled before I threw. I was like, *What just happened?* My legs didn't really recover the whole camp and preseason.

My legs may have been shot, but I was blessed by being behind Philip Rivers and Kellen Clemens at quarterback. Two great guys. In that camp, I learned more about being a quarterback than I think I learned in my entire career before that. I was in a room with so much experience. Phil had been in the league since 2004 and had spent his entire career to that point with the Chargers, making eight Pro Bowls. Kellen had been in the league since 2006, mostly as a backup. Our offensive coordinator, Ken Whisenhunt, started his NFL coaching career in 1997 and had been head coach of the Arizona Cardinals from 2007 to 2012. Quarterbacks coach Shane Steichen is now the Philadelphia Eagles' offensive coordinator.

I knew I wasn't going to push Phil or Kellen for their spots, and they couldn't have been more supportive. In our final preseason game against San Francisco, Phil and Kellen rested, so I got the start. I completed 18 of 24 passes for 158 yards. I guess I'd shown enough potential at that point that after the game, Kellen told me, "Hey, my job is to do everything in my power to get you to be the guy here eventually." Coming from Buffalo, where Tyrod and EJ were still trying to establish themselves and couldn't really be true mentors, I was blown away. It felt so nice to have veterans like that believe in me. One of the things both Phil and Kellen said to me was that they wanted me to approach the game as if I were not more athletic than they were, that what mattered most was what I did from the neck up. They told me to really prepare and study so I could beat defenses before the ball was even snapped. They said that was what they had to do because they weren't as gifted athletically as I was.

Phil's preparation was amazing. I'd actually met him before the draft. His brother Stephen worked with George Whitfield Jr. training me. One day, Phil came out to watch us and gave me some really good advice. During my interviews with teams, one question I got was whether I'd met anyone during the process who had really impressed me or whom I was starstruck by, and I said, "Phil Rivers." Getting to be his teammate, I got to see his preparation up close. His attention to detail was amazing. During preparation for one game, we were trying to figure out what the differences were between two blitzes the opponent had shown. They showed the same look, and we couldn't figure it out. Phil had to find the answer. He went back to film that was probably 10-plus years old—the film was so old that it was super grainy—to find the answer. The defensive coordinator had used that blitz that long ago, and Phil noticed that the three-technique defensive tackle's hand placement was the tell to the type of blitz it was. I was just like, *What?* It turned out that we didn't get that blitz look in the game, but it tells you how detailed Phil was in his pursuit of anything that might give him an edge. Before games, we'd draw up all the possible blitzes we'd see and protections we'd potentially call against the opponent so that nothing in the game would come as a surprise. What an education that was.

Unfortunately, I didn't get to use any of it in a game. I made the roster but was on the inactive list for every game but one. The exception was our game against, coincidentally, my old team, Buffalo, when I dressed but didn't play. We started the season 0–4, with the first two losses because of missed field goals. Rookie Younghoe

Koo, who'd beaten out veteran Josh Lambo, missed what would have been a tying 44-yard kick against the Broncos and had a 44-yarder blocked against the Dolphins that would have won the game. I'm happy that Younghoe went on to become a Pro Bowler with Atlanta, but the Chargers cut him after four games, starting a revolving door of kickers that year. It was crazy. I think we went through eight kickers.

The other crazy thing was not having home-field advantage. The Spanos family moved the team from San Diego that year, and it was not a popular move. San Diego fans were pissed. Los Angeles also got the Rams back after the franchise had spent 21 years in St. Louis, and they were the team L.A. embraced. We were like uninvited guests. We played at the StubHub Center because our stadium hadn't been built. The StubHub Center held only 27,000, and most of the spectators were fans of the visiting team. The Chargers made the move after season tickets were already sold, so San Diego fans would sell them to the opponents' fans. When we played the Eagles, their fans did the "E-A-G-L-E-S Eagles!" chants before the national anthem. I was like, *Where are we?* We got booed in our own stadium.

Despite all of the obstacles, we rebounded after our terrible start. We won three in a row after that and four in a row starting in late November but missed the playoffs with a 9–7 record.

I was content to watch and learn my first year in Los Angeles. I hoped for more after that. Then Kellen retired. They brought in Geno Smith to battle me for the backup spot in 2018 and drafted Easton Stick from North Dakota State in the fifth round. The team went with Geno over me as Phil's No. 2, and I spent the year on the practice squad. They didn't re-sign Geno after the season. In my exit interview with Coach Lynn, he said it would be my third year in the offense and I needed to step it up in 2019. He was looking for major improvement. I agreed. I attacked that off-season with the mindset that I didn't care who they brought in, the backup job was mine to lose. Three months later, they did bring someone in—Tyrod Taylor. Tyrod signed a two-year deal worth $11 million, with $6 million guaranteed the first year. With that kind of money invested in him, I knew where I stood.

Still, I worked hard during the off-season. Phil wasn't there more than once or twice a week usually. He was still living in San Diego. Tyrod and I each got reps with the ones and twos. I thought I did really well. When we got to training camp, I felt like I was killing it, just killing it. I played well in the preseason games. But by Week 3 I was not seeing any significant change in my practice reps. I asked to speak to Coach Lynn so I could get a better sense of where I stood. Who was I competing against? What was going on? I'd been told I was doing well. My completion percentage was through the roof. I felt I was putting the team in good positions and making the right checks at the line of scrimmage. I just wanted to know what their vision for me was. Coach Lynn told me to keep competing. I went into the final preseason game. Tyrod, like Phil, didn't play, which was proof that Tyrod was going to be the No. 2 quarterback. That meant I was competing with Easton Stick for a possible roster spot. We played thc 49ers and I got the start. In my four drives, we scored every time—two touchdowns and two field goals. I completed 10 of 16 passes for 149 yards and ran for 26 more. Easton Stick threw two interceptions before leading the team on a game-winning drive at the end.

I'd done everything I could do, I felt. It wasn't enough. They kept Stick and waived me on cutdown day. I was told that they wanted to trade me to get something in return, but the team that wanted me was in the division, and the Chargers didn't want me to play for a rival. The Chargers wanted to re-sign me to the practice squad, but that just felt like spinning my wheels. I thought there would be a better opportunity to be a backup elsewhere. That's actually what Coach Lynn told reporters I deserved to pursue.

A week later, Seattle claimed me on waivers. The Seahawks had Russell Wilson as their starter. Geno Smith had landed there as the backup, so I was reunited with him. It was a great room. Smart guys. But my stay didn't last long. The Seahawks had some injuries on the offensive line, and I was cut to make room for a new lineman. Seattle said they wanted to bring me back in a couple weeks when they had a roster spot.

Then the XFL came calling. The XFL was a reboot of a league that Vince McMahon from the WWE founded in 2001. The original league lasted only a year, but there were high hopes for the new version. The new XFL had eight teams in major markets that, except for St. Louis, had NFL teams. Even though I'd be making less in the XFL than even on an NFL practice squad—$150,000—the XFL would give me a chance to prove myself on the field. That was something that was looking unlikely in the NFL, at least in the short term. I was allocated to the DC Defenders in Washington, DC.

Pep Hamilton was our coach, and players got together in Louisiana to try to develop some chemistry before our training camp in Florida early in 2020. The season started on February 8 with a 31–19 win over the Seattle Dragons. I threw for 235 yards and two touchdown passes. I also threw two touchdown passes in a win the next week over the New York Guardians. Unfortunately, that was the high point. We lost the next two games, and I threw four interceptions in the first of those.

Then in March COVID-19 hit. Everything in the world, including sports, shut down. My understanding is that the XFL really wanted to keep playing because we would have had the sports world to ourselves. College basketball's March Madness was canceled, as was the NBA, NHL, and NASCAR. The XFL even tried to bill our game against Houston as the league's championship game in case the rest of the season couldn't be played. But that hope lasted only a few days. COVID was spreading like crazy, and the league had no choice but to shut down. Our coaches told us to maintain our conditioning because they hoped the league could resume play in a couple of weeks.

I stayed in shape and had some workouts set up with NFL teams. At first, the NFL had a policy in which they could have players work out for a team if they quarantined for four days after they arrived in town, did the workout, and then left immediately afterward. I had one of those with the Raiders. I got there on a Thursday, took a COVID test, quarantined at my hotel until my workout on Tuesday, and then left. But soon after that, the NFL barred any in-person workouts. Teams would have to sign players without having them in for a tryout. In that scenario, it made sense that they'd only sign players they already knew. That certainly limited my chances.

In 2021 one person who knew me well did become an NFL head coach. Urban Meyer and I talked at the national championship game in south Florida between Ohio State and Alabama a few days before he became head coach of the Jacksonville Jaguars. ESPN asked me about Coach Meyer. I said he's a great coach. He's obviously very smart. But clearly, it's different coaching in the NFL than in college. I said I expected him to put the right people around him to help smooth that transition. I thought he could be successful if he changed some of his ways and techniques. Some of the ones he used in college weren't going to work with grown men. In major college football, you can coach using fear, especially back when Coach Meyer was at Ohio State and you couldn't transfer and become immediately eligible elsewhere. The rosters in college are much bigger. Coaches can recruit past you. And at 18 or 19 years old, you're really just a kid. In the pros, a lot of the players make more than the coach. Teams will get rid of a coach before they'll get rid of a player because they have more invested in the players. In the NFL, I saw guys refuse to do certain drills or make a backup do it, and the coach really couldn't do that much about it. Coach Meyer had success in every one of his college jobs, and I thought if he could adapt, he could do the same in Jacksonville. At the national title game, he told me he was going to take the Jaguars job. I told him, "Cool. Congrats. Good luck." He asked if I thought he could do it. I told him he could as long as he understood he was dealing with grown men.

I was hoping he might want to sign me. I saw him a few more times in Columbus, including at his restaurant opening. I was still working out and in good shape, and he told me, "Stay ready in case we call you," which gave me a boost of confidence that I wasn't wasting my time still pursuing the NFL. I knew that the further you're away from the game, the window for opportunity closes. But I didn't get the call. When Jacksonville signed Tim Tebow, who'd been out of football for a long time while he tried to make it as a baseball player, that was a slap in the face. Especially since Tebow was signed as a tight end, a position he'd never played before. I mean no offense to Tebow. I also understand that in north Florida, Tebow is like a god because of what he did at the University of Florida under Coach Meyer. They were trying to get a buzz around the Jaguars, who had won only one game the previous year. They were trying to sell season tickets. That stuff skyrocketed when they signed Tebow. But there were so many guys who were more deserving of the opportunity. I was pissed because even if he didn't have a real desire to have me make the team, bringing me in for a workout could have at least kept my name out there for another opportunity. I guess I could have reached out to Coach Meyer, but I didn't want to put myself in a position where I was turning to him out of need. But I thought it was total BS that I didn't even get a look. Then the stuff came out about how things were going down in Jacksonville. I was like, *Wow, it doesn't sound like he changed.*

Urban Meyer:

I wanted to give him a tryout, but there was a feeling not to in the organization. I pushed a little bit, but I didn't micromanage all of that. The general manager and the position coach, they'd come to me and I'd give my opinion, and then the GM came to a conclusion.

Chapter 22

LIFE AFTER FOOTBALL

When I left Ohio State for the NFL, I expected a better pro career, though I hope I still get another chance. If I don't, I'll consider it a failure. Some of it is due to circumstances. Fourth-round picks aren't given the keys to a franchise. You have to be in the right place at the right time and take advantage if you get your opportunity. I never really got a legitimate one. The Bills were a team in transition the year I was there. With the Chargers, I was behind a future Hall of Fame quarterback in Philip Rivers. I wasn't going to beat him out. The same in Seattle with Russell Wilson. He was in his prime when I was with the Seahawks.

My best chance to establish myself came in my second year with the Chargers. That's when Geno Smith and I competed for the backup job. I finished the preseason extremely strong, but they kept Geno instead. I remember hearing that somebody would pick me up on the waiver wire when I got cut. But nobody did. To this day, I don't know why. It still bothers me that I never got a real opportunity because I see quarterbacks get and blow them all the time. And yet they keep getting recycled. I'll admit that it's been hard to watch the NFL since I've been out of it, especially in the preseason when you see guys you know you're better than get signed and have an opportunity to play. Some of these guys have shown they can't play. I'm not saying I've proven that I can, but I haven't shown that I can't. In 2021 I couldn't even get a workout. In May 2022 I did get another chance, with the Edmonton Elks of the CFL. An opportunity opened there because—how crazy is this?—J. T. Barrett was with them and tore his Achilles tendon. But my stay in Edmonton was a short one. The Elks released me after only two weeks. I'm not sure why. I thought I was playing well.

On September 29, 2022, I turned 30. That's an age when athletes need to be thinking about transitioning to a post-playing career. I think my transition has been unique, with one foot in football and the other in several other avenues. I haven't been with a team during the season for a couple of years, but I'm not yet willing to give up on my dream because I know I'm still capable of playing. I've been trying to strike that happy medium between staying in football shape while not letting non-football opportunities pass me by. I think I've had a pretty good balance with it.

I earned my license to sell life insurance and I've started working with former Buckeyes linebacker Ryan Shazier in that field. After his career-ending spinal injury when he was with the Pittsburgh Steelers, Ryan started an insurance company with plans to expand across the country. There's a possibility that I might eventually run his Columbus office.

I also have a gym that I opened with Eric Lichter. Eric was the head strength coach under Jim Tressel at Ohio State. When Urban Meyer came to Ohio State, he brought in his confidant Mickey Marotti. During the NFL off-season, Fox Sports asked me to tape a segment on workouts. Not long before that, I happened to bump into Eric at a movie theater. I asked Eric if he would help me with the Fox Sports spot. He did, and it went so well that I asked him to come out of retirement to help train me for good.

He talked to his wife, and they agreed that Eric should jump back into the business. In 2018 we cofounded Plus 2 and opened our first gym in suburban Columbus the next year. Eric runs the gym on a day-to-day basis, though I do some training of athletes.

> *Eric Lichter:*
>
> *It's funny that I'm partners with Cardale because I always said I'd never go into business with professional athletes. They've been pampered. They're used to people removing obstacles from them. I don't think many of them understand the value of a dollar. But Cardale is so different.*
>
> *He's definitely a smart guy. He knows the value of things. He surrounds himself with good people. He's accountable and responsible. And he's got a big heart for kids. He loves to make people smile, and he's humble.*
>
> *In his role, he really is an ambassador. He's the face of the company. He loves to come through and rub elbows and high-five and mess with the athletes. And they love him. The high school kids, when they see him, they go, "Oh my God, that's Cardale Jones," and "Oh my God, he's working out with me," and "Oh my God, he's talking shit to me." They love him. He brings a real fun demeanor and atmosphere to the company. The kids can't believe that he's so genuine and engaging. He also works with the quarterbacks and provides some skill work for them.*

He's brought value to the company in other ways. We had to get a city permit to build a concrete foundation over a dock ramp. We were having trouble finding the right contractors until Cardale used his network to find a couple that could get it done.

The other thing I've gotten involved with is something I never would have predicted. When I was at Ohio State, NCAA rules prevented us from profiting from our name, image, and likeness. The 2010 tattoo and memorabilia scandal that ended star quarterback Terrelle Pryor's OSU career and ruined the 2011 season, well, those players were just ahead of their time. As running back Boom Herron said, "Scandal is the new normal." In 2021, after losing several lawsuits related to NIL rights, the NCAA finally allowed players to profit from their status as college athletes.

If you'd told me in early 2021 that I'd be involved with NIL, I'd have said, "No freaking way." When the Ohio state legislature took up the issue, a friend of mine, Brian Schottenstein, reached out to me. I met Brian on a Buckeye Cruise for Cancer, a big fundraising event for Ohio State. We were at the casino one night sitting next to each other. Lady Luck was not on my side that night, so after I'd lost my money, we went upstairs and hung out. After the cruise ended, I continued building my friendship with him and the rest of his family, which is a prominent one in Columbus. Brian is friends with Niraj Antani, a state senator who introduced and pushed for the Ohio NIL bill. I testified, along with OSU athletic director Gene Smith and head football coach Ryan Day, on behalf of the legislation, which passed in June 2021.

In my testimony, I said I wasn't there to advocate for star football players. They're going to get plenty of money from NIL. I said I was there because I wanted others to get their share, players who wouldn't have pro careers or athletes in Olympic sports. I used

J. T. as an example. After a great career at Ohio State, he bounced around on NFL practice squads for a few years but never found a home. He's now working his way up as a coach with the Detroit Lions. J. T. could have made life-changing money from NIL at Ohio State.

I think about how much players from our 2014 and 2015 teams could have made from NIL. It's crazy. Ryan Day said that it would take $13 million in NIL to keep a championship-level roster intact. I think it would have taken at least $30 million to keep ours together if the transfer portal had been in existence then. Think about the quarterbacks—me, J. T., and Braxton. It would have taken a significant amount of money to keep any of us from leaving.

Then think about all the other stars we had. Joey Bosa. Zeke. Vonn Bell. Mike Thomas. Eli Apple. Joshua Perry, a Columbus guy. Darron Lee, another Columbus guy. Dontre Wilson. Curtis Samuel. Michael Bennett. Adolphus Washington. Tyvis. Doran Grant. Jeff Heuerman. Devin Smith. Evan Spencer. Jalin Marshall. The whole offensive line, especially local guys Jacoby Boren and Pat Elflein and future first-round picks Taylor Decker and Billy Price. Then there were all the young guys, such as Raekwon McMillan and the incoming freshmen. We might have broken the bank.

There's no way to know how much I personally could have made from NIL if it had been around when I played. I think that now, a starting Ohio State quarterback who isn't even a star, just a guy who is more of a caretaker, would make $800,000 at a minimum. But these days, you have to be a star to be the starting quarterback at Ohio State the way the offense has evolved. A Heisman Trophy candidate who could lead OSU to a national championship would add another $2 to $3 million to that.

People have asked if I'm envious of the NIL money that current players are making. Absolutely not. My feeling is that you always enter a place on the backs of those who came before you.

When I trained at the Woody and benefited from the facility and the great people there, I'd done nothing to create that. That was all there because of the Rose Bowls and Big Ten titles and national championships won by my predecessors. I had nothing to do with that success. I feel I owe it to people who came after me at Ohio State to do what I can to leave it even better than it was when I arrived. Besides, I'm not an envious or jealous person.

> *J. T. Barrett:*
>
> *I haven't thought about it a lot, but people bring that up to me, how much we might have made if NIL had been around. That would have been cool, but I knew how I was without money, so who knows how I would have been with dollars in my pocket? I am OK that NIL wasn't around for me. I have no bitterness.*
>
> *But those 2014–15 teams were one of the hottest things around, definitely in college football. There were a lot of heavy hitters—not myself but Zeke, Braxton, Bosa, Mike Thomas. We had crazy-talented young players running down on the kickoff team, like Jerome Baker and Denzel Ward. We had Marshon Lattimore and Gareon Conley. A lot of us would have made a lot of money.*

Three months after NIL went into effect, through some people I met at the statehouse, I was asked about helping with starting an agency. It just so happened that athletes were hitting me up for opportunities and advice I might be able to give them. I saw a few of the contracts that some of them had already signed, and the percentages they were giving up to their representatives were insane. They were getting screwed.

I teamed with Dave DeVillers, Mehek Cooke, and Jordan Ohler to create Ten Talents NIL, a marketing agency that helps athletes get name, image, and likeness opportunities. We don't represent Ohio State athletes exclusively. We have football players at Penn State and Cincinnati. We have a softball player at Ohio University. The message I share with student-athletes is that their name, image, and likeness are things they own and are responsible for, on and off the field. They can hurt their NIL opportunities with what they do off the field as much as they can help it with what they do on the field. We help teach them how to be their own business, and that everything really is a part of business. These athletes are at a critical age. Sometimes it's hard to explain to a 17- or 18-year-old that the game they've played for fun as a kid will now become a business, for better and worse. The pure joy of playing will fade because they're entering a multimillion-dollar enterprise. It's not necessarily fair, but it is what they're signing up for. They have to do what's best for their brand and their career. They need to understand that coaches will do that as well. Coaches will leave for a better job and opportunity. If your position coach is offered a coordinator job or head coaching job, you better believe he's going to take it, so you have to do what's right for your own career too.

Obviously, I experienced that with Tom Herman leaving for Houston. My own Ohio State career is a testament to how college can make or break you. I went from feeling I could walk down High Street naked without being noticed early in my career to drawing a crowd and being stopped everywhere I went after the 2014 national championship. Before J. T. Barrett got hurt, you couldn't find my No. 12 jersey anywhere in a store. They probably didn't even make them. Then after that championship, everywhere you turned, there was a No. 12 jersey. I got nothing from the sale of those. All these companies were coming out with 12 GAUGE T-shirts and all this other stuff. Of course, I would have loved to have been able to take advantage of that.

Back then, when I was driving my 2006 Dodge Charger Dale-mobile, I could have used that money. Tyvis and I knew how to live frugally because neither of us came from families with money. During the academic year, it wasn't so tough because we got scholarship checks. It was harder to save in the summer when we didn't. I was in school when the NCAA finally allowed athletes to start getting cost-of-attendance checks that helped cover living expenses beyond room, board, and tuition. In-state students got less than those who were from out of state, but that extra $200 or so went a long way. We felt like we were rich, or at least not poor. But it clearly wasn't life-changing money the way that NIL can make stars rich. That kind of money can set up not just the players but give financial security to their families. That's a huge deal when you realize that the NFL is no given, and that few players have long careers even if they make it to the league.

When I'm attracting athletes to Ten Talents NIL, I don't think of it as recruiting. I consider myself as playing more of a big brother role. These kids were young when I played at Ohio State, but they know who I am, and their families certainly know who I am. That helps, because there's an instant level of familiarity. But I'm up front with them that I don't work for Ohio State. I don't pretend OSU is the greatest place in the world for everyone. I don't sugar-coat anything, and I never lie to them. I tell the athletes that they're going to control their destiny no matter where they go.

It's such a critical, vulnerable time for kids. They're getting recruited by people who are experienced in the process and know how to push all the right buttons. They're just teenagers trying to find their way in life and deciding where the best place is to spend the next three to five years and reach their goals athletically, academically, and career-wise. Unless there's an older sibling who's been through it, his family is feeling its way through the recruiting process. My role is to be honest and helpful. I'll tell them the opportunities that NIL might provide. I'll also explain that their athletic career might not work out for them. I've seen more guys who didn't pan out than did, even among big-time recruits.

I'm also involved in a separate NIL-related enterprise, the Foundation. Brian Schottenstein and I started that. With the Foundation, we don't represent players. We deal with player engagement. We provide opportunities for our student-athletes to invest their name, image, and likeness with our charitable partners. We educate OSU recruits and their families about our mission at the Foundation and how we provide NIL opportunities to current student-athletes. Every dollar we raise through the Foundation goes to the student-athletes.

Eric Lichter:

The greatest skill Cardale Jones has is that he is a frickin' chameleon. He can change his stripes. He can sit in a boardroom at the Foundation and be talking to donors wanting to write a check for $10 million. He could be sitting in a boardroom of a Fortune 100 company and could handle himself well there. He could be on the streets of Cleveland where it's a war zone and crack cocaine is being dealt, and he would be able to relate and be able to navigate that. And he can do everything in between. He's just a people person through and through and knows how to connect with people. He connects with people better than anyone I've ever seen.

I agree with that 100 percent. I do find myself being able to fit in with different groups of people and being relatable. There wouldn't be a room full of people or a conversation that I would feel uncomfortable participating in or being around. I've said this many times: If you don't like me or if you have a problem with me, you've probably got problems yourself. I have so many different friends from different backgrounds, religious beliefs, social views, financial statuses. I can go from hanging out with some big shot at Jeff Ruby's Steakhouse to going into a McDonald's and having a great time. I just think it comes with not wanting to make someone uncomfortable around me. If I don't know something, I'm not ashamed to say, "I don't know." Like with politics. I'm not afraid to say I'm not educated enough on that topic to give you a valid two cents. One of my favorite sayings is, "It's better to remain silent and be thought a fool than to speak and remove all doubt." Coach Herman used to tell me that, and I didn't know then if that was good or bad. Now I know.

Urban Meyer:

I think Cardale is really smart. I think he's brilliant. When he locks in on something. I think he's brilliant. I witnessed it. From Wisconsin to the national championship game, I would say brilliant with a capital B.

I don't know why he called me brilliant. But in my own way I do think I'm extremely smart. I just have a different way of commanding a room, a different way of leading, a different way of understanding things. Like in football, I was never really taught the X's and O's until college. In high school, it was really just dropping back and looking for an open guy. But I wouldn't say it came easily to me. In college, it took time, effort, energy, and studying my butt off. That ramped up even more at the next level, even if I never really got a chance to show what I could do. I just understood there was more than one way to get the results you want, and I think I understand what works best for me, even if it's not always the conventional way.

That's what I'm doing professionally as of 2023. Personally, I'm quite busy as well. I'm very involved in helping to raise my three kids, who all live in the Cleveland area. Their moms do a great job with them. I have a good co-parenting partnership with them. As with any relationship, we have our ups and downs, especially since my kids are in different households. Sometimes their moms and I disagree about things, which is to be expected. But there are more ups than downs, which I'm extremely grateful for.

Chloe, Carter, and Owen are great kids. They're all different in their own ways, but I definitely see myself in all of them. Chloe is the boss. I wouldn't say she is starting to know how to play her parents against each other, but she knows who to ask for what. She knows how to get what she wants at times by saying certain things. But she's also very giving and nice. She doesn't want to hurt anyone's feelings. Chloe will do things for her friends or cousins or brothers that she might not necessarily want to do but will go along with them because she knows they might want to.

Carter is the sweetest kid ever. Super big heart. Super nice. I know he's going to be like me in that he'll give someone his last dollar. I think he's the most generous of the three. He's crazy about Chloe. Whenever I get him, he'll ask, "Are we going to get Chloe? Are we hanging out with Chloe?"

Owen is into every sport you can think of—hockey, wrestling, baseball, basketball, flag football. Super busy. Into a lot of different things. In what's a testament to his mom, Morgan, he's always been smarter than his age. As soon as he was able to talk, you could have a real conversation with him.

Even though I'm about two hours away from them since I live in Columbus, it's very important to me to be heavily involved in my kids' lives. The fact that I didn't have a father and my mother had issues reinforces that. It's not easy, especially with kids from three different women. It's hard not being able to be present and have an impact on their lives every day as much as I want. But it puts things in perspective too. It's inconceivable to me that a dad wouldn't want this responsibility or would bail on it. It's kind of mind-blowing. Through the good, bad, and ugly with their moms and the challenges of raising them not living in the same city, I still wouldn't trade it for the world. It's still trial and error with me as a parent. I never had a dad, so I try to do what I think I would have wanted in those situations. I don't have the example of what to do. I have to imagine the way I wish I'd been raised and parent that way. I am blessed that my kids' moms are unbelievable parents. I'm fortunate that Jeaney, Morgan, and Sabrina are faith-driven, high-character, awesome moms. They're very loving and really care about our kids' education.

I do lean on Michelle quite a bit. Our relationship continues to get stronger and stronger as we go through different things in our lives as adults. She's still my mom, and I look to her for advice. Because she lives in Cleveland and is closer to my kids, she's a huge outlet for me and kind of an extension of me when I can't be there.

You might be wondering if I've patched things up with my momma. Unfortunately, no. I sometimes wish that relationship were better. But I do believe she has some personal issues and personal growth that she needs to overcome and address before our relationship can take steps in the right direction. Do I ever see that happening? Honestly, I don't. I think it's wishful thinking. I think I'd approach that situation differently if Michelle weren't around or our relationship somehow went south. If I had no one else to be a mother figure, maybe I would try a little harder to have that relationship with my momma. But Michelle was the one I leaned on when I was younger and needed someone. She was there for me. So naturally I built a relationship with her. The lack of a relationship I have with my momma is not something I'm eager to fix because I don't believe it's my fault. I've taken steps in the past to try to talk to her about things or try to get down to the nitty-gritty of why things turned out the way they did, and I feel those conversations kind of went nowhere.

My life has come full circle in some ways. In December 2022 I watched Glenville finally win the state title on the same field at the Pro Football Hall of Fame in Canton where we were denied 11 years earlier when we lost to Hilliard Davidson. I was so happy for Ted Ginn Sr. He'd beaten enormous odds just to be alive after he was diagnosed with pancreatic cancer several years ago. I attribute his survival to his willpower, his faith, and his mission. He believed his journey was not done yet. The program had gone through some lean years before Coach Ginn brought it back. Some of the players he coached in his early years are now coaches on his staff.

I took my 10-year-old cousin Jabrie to the state championship game. We visited the team in the locker room a couple hours before kickoff. I put athletic tape on some of the players and shared a few words of wisdom to inspire them to accomplish what my team didn't. Jabrie was on cloud nine in the locker room being with the players. It reminded me of when I was with the Glenville Titans and idolized the high school players who seemed so old to me. Jabrie was telling me, "I'm playing here! I'm gonna come here!" To see that spark lit was cool. He ran onto the field with the team. It was a cold night, and I was bundled up head to toe in a hunting outfit. I was worried about Jabrie being cold. All he had was a jacket and some sweatpants. But I think he was oblivious to the weather. He was running around on the sideline like a bat out of hell. He even became the water boy. I don't know how he became the water boy, but everybody, including his mom, was texting me after seeing him on TV. And he corrected me when I referred to him as the water boy. "No, I'm the water *man*," he said.

I've mentioned my nephew D'Shawntae Jones, who's Glenville's running back. I've watched him his whole career, and he told me some of the things he wants to do are because of me. I enjoyed watching his confidence grow. He didn't play as a freshman because it was the COVID year, and I knew the transition to playing varsity as a sophomore would be a challenge. He was going from playing with kids to playing against guys closer to being men. I stressed to him that he had to understand how different it would be. The physicality of the game and the mental side of the game would be much harder. He needed to grow, and he did. I've helped train him, and he's already gotten some good Division I offers.

Watching Jabrie and D'Shawntae brought back so many memories of when I was a kid dreaming of overcoming my background. I know others had it worse than I did. Even if my parental and economic situations were not ideal, I had siblings and other relatives who helped me. I had several coaches and mentors, especially Ted Ginn Sr., who helped steer me right when I started to veer off track. Most of all, I had Michelle. I hope my story serves as inspiration for kids who can identify with it.

In some ways, it's hard to believe it's been so many years since our national championship. I'm still recognized almost everywhere I go in Columbus. That's partly because of my size. People notice this big dude and then realize who they're looking at. Often they'll strike up a conversation. I'm happy to engage with anyone, though I'd sometimes prefer not to if I'm at a restaurant with my kids and want some privacy.

Some people might think I'm really gregarious and outgoing, but I don't think I necessarily am. But I do think I'm relatable. My mistakes have been in public view. The first time most people heard of me was my infamous tweet. I still have more than 1.5 million followers on Twitter. I suspect many of those follow me because they're waiting for me to tweet something stupid again. I don't think I do, but I don't try to be overly careful on Twitter, either. At this point in my life, I am who I am. When I was in college, I tried to conform to the mold that others expected me to fit into. Urban Meyer and Tom Herman believed a quarterback had to conduct himself in a certain way. I tried to be the straight-and-narrow quarterback. It just wasn't me. I learned that it's not worth it looking in the mirror and not recognizing yourself. I've said that about other aspects of my life when I've had to change or fit in or accommodate so much. Don't get me wrong, I naturally adapt to different situations well. I hope to continue to learn and grow as I enter my thirties and beyond. But I never lose sight of who I really am.

It's been a remarkable ride so far. I've experienced plenty of tough times. So many times as a kid in Cleveland, my life could have gone off the rails or even ended. At Ohio State, I barely hung in until I got my chance. I think that's why some people identify with me. They know what it's like to struggle. They believe in themselves but are just waiting for a chance to shine. That I got mine and we won a championship resonates with people. I've said plenty of times that I don't think I even played particularly well in those three postseason games. I was fortunate that my teammates rose to the occasion around me. Together, we all got to experience something magical on a national stage that few ever do. That things didn't go as well as I would have liked in 2015 or in the NFL is all part of that too. We all know how fleeting success can be. But I'm proud of what I've accomplished and proud of the person I've become. I have persevered. My first 30 years have been quite a journey. I believe I'm bound for great things in my future, and I'm so excited for that journey.